PRAISE FOR
ALL-CAPS YOU

I think something that speaks so well of Emma and really says all you need to know about her is in the dedication of this book. She dedicates this book to the Lord, and the first thing she calls Him is "friend." Emma is friends with God. She walks so closely with Him and lives her life with an acute awareness of His presence. That awareness of His presence and knowledge of what that means for her life fills her with the most sincere joy and confidence, and she longs to share with the world. In this book she wants to tell you about her friend and how He desires a relationship with each of us—a relationship abounding in love, hope, and joy.

MARY KATE ROBERTSON, blogger

Emma Mae carries a contagious joy that radiates from the pages of this book. She packs a positive punch with encouraging and insightful ways to let God's truth settle deep in our hearts. You'll be forever changed by this 30-day adventure!

REBEKAH LYONS, bestselling author of *Rhythms of Renewal* and *You Are Free*

Original from start to finish, *ALL-CAPS YOU*, written by lifelong sister and friend, Emma Jenkins, is not just a devotional, it's a daily morning cup of coffee with a friend who will hold up the mirror for you to see yourself exactly as you are: a deeply loved, God-purposed child of the King.

SADIE ROBERTSON HUFF, author of *Live Fearless*, host of Live Original podcast

The way that the Spirit's wisdom and truth effortlessly flow from Emma is astounding. Her genuine joy and love for God reaps a newfound confidence, hope, and thirst to know God intimately in this book. These are the words of a world changer, and they are worth storing up in one's heart!

KIRBY MINNICK, speaker, YouTuber, host of Bought + Beloved podcast

In a culture where our confidence is measured by likes on Instagram and comparison increases with every post we look at, it's easy to allow our identity to be consumed by popularity, appearance, and following. In *ALL-CAPS YOU*, Emma Mae Jenkins fights against the current of culture, and reclaims our purpose and identity as sons and daughters of the Most High King. Not only does Emma speak these words boldly, but she lives them out faithfully for the Kingdom's sake, instead of conforming for the world's sake.

GABRIELLE ODOM, HowToLife movement speaker, Initiative Network core team member

As always, Emma uses Scripture, real life application, and her exuberant joy through her words to capture readers' hearts. In the pages of this devotional, you will come away encouraged, enlightened, and spurred on in whatever season you're in. Get your heart (and pen) ready to experience the love and grace of Jesus in *ALL-CAPS YOU*.

LAUREN FAITH McROBERTS, blogger, social media personality, author of *Living Out Transparent Faith*

ALL-CAPS YOU makes you want to dance, sing, and truly LIVE in ALL CAPS. Emma Mae is a true ray of the Lord's light. Her obedient writing voice takes people of all ages to the heart of their childlike faith, opening their spirit to the Father's arms willingly through this conversational devotional.

GEORGIA BROWN, influencer, host of Faith & Friends podcast

Emma Mae continues to shine the light of Christ on others in her newest book *ALL-CAPS YOU*. Her ability to make studying God's Word attainable and fun for teenagers and young adults is remarkable. In *ALL-CAPS YOU* she asks the reader to join her in a thought-provoking and Christ-centered journey into their own hearts . . . and it's a beautiful journey!

MINDY McKNIGHT, author of *Viral Parenting*, founder of Hairitage by Mindy

Emma speaks with confidence and passion about the Word of God. With power and true conviction, she leads the reader toward the heart of God with every word. You will not regret walking through this devotional!

CHELSEA CROCKETT, author of *Above All Else*, actress, YouTuber

ALL-CAPS YOU

A 30-Day Adventure toward
Finding Joy in Who God Made You to Be

Emma Mae Jenkins

wander
An imprint of
Tyndale House
Publishers

Visit Tyndale online at tyndale.com.

Visit the author's website at emmamaejenkins.com.

TYNDALE and Tyndale's quill logo are registered trademarks of Tyndale House Publishers. *Wander* and the Wander logo are trademarks of Tyndale House Publishers. Wander is an imprint of Tyndale House Publishers, Carol Stream, Illinois.

ALL-CAPS YOU: A 30-Day Adventure toward Finding Joy in Who God Made You to Be

Designed by Eva M. Winters

Edited by Deborah King

For information about special discounts for bulk purchases, please contact Tyndale House Publishers at csresponse@tyndale.com, or call 1-800-323-9400.

ISBN 978-1-4964-4026-6

Printed in the United States of America

26	25	24	23	22	21	20
7	6	5	4	3	2	1B

I am dedicating this book to the Lord—
my Friend, my Savior, my King, my Beloved.
He is worthy, and it is by Him, through Him,
and for Him that we can live in ALL CAPS.

CONTENTS

FOREWORD

Emma Mae Jenkins is a breath of fresh air. When I see someone younger who loves Jesus so sincerely and wants to teach His Word, it brings me so much excitement for the future. I was blessed to visit with Emma, and her passion in person is the same as on these pages: all she wants is for you to know and love her God and to experience the joy and delight He has given to her in your own life.

Some people look around and see the days getting darker, but I look around and see the days getting brighter. All of YOU in your places wanting to love God and wanting to make a difference in people's lives. This is the short life we've been given, and let's make the very most of it together. These pages will help in that journey.

JENNIE ALLEN, author of *Get Out of Your Head*,
founder and visionary of IF:Gathering

INTRODUCTION

When the words of the world come knocking at our door, it is very easy to tune in and give them our full attention—but these words always leave us feeling empty, unsatisfied, not pretty enough, or questioning our worth. On the other hand, the voice of the Lord never leads us astray. He is faithful to His Word, and so when He says that we are beautiful and that He will never let us down and that we are more than conquerors through His Son, these are words that we can confidently trust.

To live in ALL CAPS is to give attention and to tune into the words that God has spoken, even when the words of the world sound loud. In the Lord we lack no good thing. We are fully loved, fully chosen, and fully known by God, and therefore we can fully be who He has called us to be—we can truly live our lives in ALL CAPS. When God first gave me the dream to write this book, my heart was to share with you that the Lord has uniquely and purposefully handcrafted each of you—and you were meant to walk in this joyful truth. My vision is to see you walk in an intimate relationship with Jesus because it is only in an intimate relationship with Him that you can fully be who you were made to be.

In every aspect of life, whether it be approval, friendships, trials, appearance, or thoughts, when God's Word is guiding our steps, we can discover the joy of who He made us to be in all aspects. He desires for us to live abundantly, and it is only when we abide in Him that we can live as He desires.

I pray that this book encourages you to grow in love with God and the words that He speaks, and as you grow in love with who He is, may you grow in love with who you are in Him—and walk in that with boldness.

Emma Mae Jenkins

CHOOSE to listen to His VOICE.

BREAK THE MOLD

Do not conform to the pattern of this world,
but be transformed by the renewing of your mind.
Then you will be able to test and approve what God's
will is—his good, pleasing and perfect will.

ROMANS 12:2

The World's Mold

Going to check my phone, I take a deep breath, fearful of the messages I may find there.

> *Your eyebrows look like caterpillars.*
> *You've been brainwashed into believing in Jesus.*
> *Your singing makes my ears bleed.*
> *You're too over the top.*
> *You don't have to love Jesus that much.*
> *You're crazy.*

My appearance has been criticized. My smile has been ridiculed. My faith has been mocked publicly. Tears burn my eyes as the voices shout their perverted, unkind, and disrespectful statements. On some occasions, I have taken a second look in the mirror, finding myself for a moment questioning my worth. Even if these words are not accurate, I can begin to believe them if I don't know what is true. I can feel like I need to conform to the mold the world tells me I should fit into. Pleasing people can become my focus, tempting me to compromise instead of being the free, unique, and beautiful me that God called me to be.

The hateful words still ring loud and clear, but I ask God to quiet my heart with His love.

In what ways do you see yourself trying to fit the mold? How does this hold you back from being who God made you to be?

• Comparing myself to others—
Holds me back from being
the person He fearfully &
wonderfully made me to be;
and find myself living in
fear often.

The voices that we listen to will determine the path we take. God made us to do great things, live abundantly, and bring Him glory, but this can only happen when we choose to listen to His voice. The Bible says we have an enemy—Satan—and that his native language is lies (John 8:44). He is a liar who wants us to believe we need to be prettier, stronger, faster, smarter, cooler. The devil wants us to believe that everyone is supposed to like us and that we need to work harder until they do. Every second, the enemy works to keep us down, to keep us feeling like we're never going to be good enough. He wants us to feel like we must strive to be approved. His twisted mind-set will hold us back from being the beautiful people God knitted us together so purposefully to be (Psalm 139:13-14).

Sometimes, I forget that the real me does not need to be ashamed. I am loved unconditionally, already approved by God. Satan knows that if he can deceive me into believing that my worth is found in what others say about me, then I will miss out on the truth of who I am because of whose I am. Instead, I choose to fill my heart with what God says about me and filter the negative through God's truth. His Word equips me, and His Spirit empowers me for every good work He's planned for me (2 Timothy 3:16-17). But to walk in His truth, I must spend time daily nourishing my soul with His Word as I rest in His constant presence.

When I am tempted to conform to the opinions and demands of others, I can choose to cling to the words of God that I have chosen to hide in my heart (Psalm 119:11).

What voices are you listening to? What does God say about you?

1. My parents, family, friends, (maybe) social media

2. God says that I am fearfully & wonderfully made, and that I am so loved by Him. He will NEVER leave my side.

Romans 12:2 tells us, "<u>Do not conform to the pattern of this world</u>, but be transformed by the renewing of your mind. Then you will be able to test and approve what God's will is—his good, pleasing, and perfect will." <u>To conform is to "fit the mold of"</u> something acceptable or predetermined. The patterns of this world include whatever feels good, whatever keeps us from avoiding being singled out, whatever is against God's best for us.

What is the opposite of conforming? To transform. To reshape, rebuild, or rearrange. When we submit ourselves to God, a reshaping of our thought process begins to take place, just like a caterpillar transforming into a stunning butterfly. Because God loves me so much, He is willing to meet me where I am, but He loves me too much to leave me there. By standing on God's Word, we have the authority to abolish every deceiving pattern that the enemy might have crafted to destroy our uniqueness and distract us from the life God designed us to live. Fitting in truly wasn't meant to be our goal. <u>God has set us apart.</u>

The beautiful process of hearing, believing, and obeying God's Word so we can begin living out who God called us to be is called transformation, and it doesn't happen overnight. Through the journey of daily discovering who He is and who we are in Him, we begin to seek what God says about us, and the rebuilding, reshaping, and renewing starts to take place. Delighting in His truth, we can joyfully be the people God created us to be. Like a caterpillar, we were made to be transformed. We were made to soar in God's will, even when the world is going the other way (Isaiah 40:31). It's time to turn away from letting our identity be rooted in who the world says we are.

It's time to break the mold and embrace the joy of living all caps for God.

What does your alone time with God look like daily? How is He transforming you this week, month, year?

My usual alone time with God consists of praying to him, and reading short, daily devotionals whenever I can. For this week, month, AND year, He is transforming me to conspire in the Word

_more by also including
bible study, devotional
readings (like this), and
listening to podcasts
presenting the Word of
God._

DEAR GOD. I TRUST THAT YOU ARE WHO YOU SAY
YOU ARE AND THAT I AM WHO YOU SAY I AM. HELP ME
TO WALK IN YOUR TRUTH NO MATTER WHAT LIES OTHERS SAY
TO SHAKE UP MY CONFIDENCE. HELP ME TO BE
TRANSFORMED BY YOUR WORD.

GOD made each & every ONE of US a limited EDITION.

STAY IN YOUR LANE

*Before I formed you in the womb I knew you,
before you were born I set you apart.*

JEREMIAH 1:5

The Comparison Trap

One day my lovely sister and I were driving home from school. A car pulled out in front of us and headed straight for us. They didn't realize they were in the wrong lane. In urgency, to let them know and keep us safe, I honked my horn. Truly seconds later, I questioned if I was the one who had drifted into the wrong lane. I actually said out loud, "Wait! Am I in the right lane?" I doubted myself because something was coming at me from the other direction.

Doesn't that reflect our spiritual journey sometimes? When we are running the race that God has called us to run, following His purpose, the enemy will throw flaming arrows of fear or doubt or pride straight at our hearts (Ephesians 6:16). We can find ourselves wondering if the truth is actually true. We begin to wonder if we are in the right lane. We begin to doubt the worth of the abilities and gifts that God has entrusted to us. When we are not prepared for attacks from the enemy, the flaming arrow of insecurity often leads to a response of comparison. We don't feel like we're enough. We don't feel like we measure up. We don't trust who God says we are.

Sometimes I forget who I am in Christ and start to believe that I am not worthy. In those times, I begin to compare all that I am to others. This is a dangerous place to be because comparison is not a part of God's design. He made each and every one of us an original. Each of us is a limited edition. The enemy wants us to compare ourselves to others, in hopes that we will miss the radiant and abundant joy of "driving" in a manner worthy of the unique calling we have each received from the Lord. Comparison diverts our attention from God. We can be stopped dead in our lane simply because our path doesn't look the same as the person driving next to us.

Many have heard the saying "Comparison is the thief of joy." When we compare ourselves to others, we are pointing out what we don't have rather than praising God for what we do have—and we miss out on seeing the beauty in others too.

In what ways have you been tempted to compare your life to the lives of others? How can you keep your focus on God and who He created you to be?

1. My grades, my physical attributes, my personality, my overall performances (in sports, for example).

2. I need to take the time to pray for God to help me get back on my heavenly path, where there's joy.

Unique You

There is no one else on earth like me—no one else like you. Before we were born, the King of kings engraved us upon the palm of His hand (Isaiah 49:16). He was enthralled by our beauty as He delicately placed every freckle, dimple, and curve upon each sweet face. He delighted in speaking love over us and embracing us with His compassion.

The Great I Am. Oh, how I can just see Him and how He was probably weeping tears of awe because He got to call us His. He determined our height and proclaimed every inch of us flawless, from the color of our skin to the shape of our eyes, from the tone of our voice to the curliness or straightness of our hair. Our Heavenly Groom proclaimed us pure masterpieces in the presence of all creation. No question. We are treasured and made with purpose. We are set apart. We are planned. We are not accidents. Nothing about us can be considered a mistake. The Author of Humanity chose to write our names in His book before the existence of time because each and every one of us is worthy of a role in His story (Revelation 13:8). He said, "Yes, I want you." He called us by name (Isaiah 43:1). Our lives are abounding in the purpose of God. He breathed into our lungs, so that we may live the life that He intentionally planned for us to live with Him, by Him, through Him, and for Him (Genesis 2:7).

When we realize that God made us perfect, exactly how we are, we find pure confidence. We can accept ourselves and others as set apart for God's glory, rather than not good enough when compared to someone else. We will begin to see ourselves and others as God does.

How did God make you unique? What specific gifts and abilities has He blessed you with?

One of the most obvious unique things about me is the cochlear implants. And along with it, the hardship and responsibilities, which he entrusted me with it because he knew I could handle it. He blessed me with the gifts of peace, kindness, ability to care and be considerate.

Christ's Body

God didn't make us to be like the person to the left or right of us.

My wonderful daddy describes it like this: If you were to cut off your pinkie toe, even though the pinkie toe is super-duper small, you would be in pain. It would be hard to walk. In the same way, we are all together the body of Christ. We are set apart to play different roles and perform different functions. Without these varying roles, the body doesn't function how God designed. If I am a pinkie toe and compare myself to the ear all the time, I completely miss out on the set-apart purpose of helping the body balance because I am so upset that I can't hear (1 Corinthians 12:14-20).

Not only does God's lane for us have purpose, but those to the left and right of us have purpose as well. When we start to recognize one another as key parts of God's Kingdom that have been designed uniquely in unity, we can look to Jesus together. We can complement one another's beauty rather than comparing ourselves with a heart posture of insecurity.

So, beauty queens and mighty warriors, we have no need to question the lane God chooses for us. We don't need to look to the left and right or worry about comparison. With our eyes fixed on Jesus, we can keep running the race that has been set before us with endurance (Hebrews 12:1-2).

What is your part to play in the body of Christ? In what
ways can you genuinely celebrate those around you today?

1. If I was a part of the body of Christ, I would probably be the ear.

2. I can give them (endless) compliments, make treats for them, give time up to hang out with them, and just be myself.

DEAR GOD, THANK YOU FOR PURPOSEFULLY PLANNING
AND MAKING ME. HELP ME TO SEE MYSELF THE WAY THAT
YOU SEE ME SO THAT I MAY ALSO SEE OTHERS
THE WAY THAT YOU SEE OTHERS.

We are BEAUTIFUL because GOD, the CREATOR of beauty, MADE us.

FEARFULLY AND WONDERFULLY MADE

I praise you because I am fearfully and wonderfully made; your works are wonderful, I know that full well.

PSALM 139:14

A Father's Love

Right before my first day of high school, I walked into my bathroom to see a note written by my dad that was taped to the mirror. The note said,

> Emma,
>
> Nothing in a makeup bag could make you any more beautiful than you are today. A beautiful heart makes a beautiful woman. Not sure how I could love you more than I do today.
>
> Love,
> Daddy

I still have this note on my mirror. When I look at it, my heart is filled with joy and honor for my dad. He not only thinks about me, but he loves me unconditionally for who I am.

My dad reflects the heart of our heavenly Father so well. God thinks about us all of the time (Psalm 139:17-18). The love of God is so real and so strong. In His presence, I feel overwhelmed with joy. My heart is consumed with awe at the thought of Him wanting to be with me.

Zephaniah 3:17 says that "He will take great delight in you; . . . [he] will rejoice over you with singing."

Who, me?

Yes.

In the midst of my being overwhelmed in the inexpressible and glorious joy of being His, God is rejoicing with singing at the simple thought of me.

How have you experienced God's unconditional love? How does it make you feel?

I have experienced God's unconditional love through the people that he put in my life. Whenever I am feeling so depressed, the people in my life help me see joy and love again. I realized that it was God's work all along.

Priceless Worth

The Lord made us with respect, honor, and awe. He is enthralled by our beauty and delights in calling us His.

This becomes harder and harder to believe the more that we accept what other people say and confuse someone else's opinions with our true identity. In this world, from social media to movies, magazines to society, we hear that we are beautiful *if*—if we are this tall, this size, this skin tone. Only if we have this voice, this smile. As culture changes and shifts, standards and expectations of beauty change too. So many of us determine what we wear, how we talk, who we hang out with, based on society's ever-changing definition of beauty. In doing this, we will never be content with who we are or who we're pretending to be. As the world's standards change, we become worn out and restless by constantly trying to prove our own value.

All the while, the King of kings has already determined our priceless worth before the world even existed. God says we are fearfully and wonderfully made (Psalm 139:14). God says we are valuable (Matthew 10:29-31). God says He made us beautiful exactly as we are. Still, even though we hear His words, we aren't always quick to believe the truth fully because the world is telling us the exact opposite. If our focus is on the world, it doesn't matter how many times we hear what's true because we believe and follow whatever we are focused on. But the more time we spend with God, the more quickly and easily we begin to hear and acknowledge His voice.

What does God say about you? How is it different from what the world says?

What God says about me is that I am already perfect in his eyes, and to not be afraid to speak His truth. However, the world says the opposite.

God's Workmanship

What if instead of believing the lies of the devil, we choose to receive what God has said? What if we believe the truth that never changes or shifts, the truth that assures us we are priceless? Ephesians 2:10 says, "We are his workmanship, created in Christ Jesus for good works, which God prepared beforehand, that we should walk in them" (ESV). God's truth declares we are beautiful because God, the creator of beauty, made us. Our smiles can be genuine and our confidence steady because our souls know our true worth in God's eyes.

When our souls grasp the precious truth that we are God's wonderful workmanship, we can believe we are made with uniqueness and purpose. We can begin to have a steadfast confidence, even in the midst of the shifting standards of the world. When we see ourselves the way that God sees us, the burden of striving to be enough begins to fade. A joyfully different perspective will take its rightful place in our hearts. When we look in the mirror, the truth of who God says we are will lead us to remember that He is thinking about us and loves us unconditionally. The changing standards of culture cannot consume us when we choose to believe that we are what God says we are . . . fearfully and wonderfully made.

What does it mean to you to be fearfully and wonderfully made? How are you going to walk in that truth today?

1. Despite knowing that sin will always be there, God still fearfully and wonderfully made him to bring light to the world.

2. I walk in the truth by being confident in myself; to not be afraid to walk with my head held high for what I believe? God.

DEAR GOD, THANK YOU FOR SEEING ME AND KNOWING ME FULLY—AND STILL LOVING ME FULLY. THANK YOU FOR FEARFULLY AND WONDERFULLY MAKING ME. YOUR WORD IS TRUE AND UNCHANGING. HELP ME TO CHOOSE TO KEEP THIS AT THE FOREFRONT OF MY THOUGHTS WHEN I LOOK IN THE MIRROR AND AM CONFRONTED WITH SHIFTING STANDARDS.

THE RIGHT TIME IS NOW

*Don't let anyone look down on you because
you are young, but set an example for the believers in
speech, in conduct, in love, in faith and in purity.*

1 TIMOTHY 4:12

The Older Crowd

Have you ever felt like you needed to wait until you become a little older to serve as a leader? Or maybe you have looked up to people who are older than you and thought, *I cannot wait to live boldly and make a difference like they do when I am that age.* I know that I have personally looked up to role models of mine and thought that once I was the age they are, then I could make more of an impact as they do.

But something so beautiful that I have realized is that God made me to be a light for His glory, lead in His love, encourage in His truth, speak up to protect the weak, be a peacemaker, and walk closely with Him *today.* Looking up to those who are further ahead in the journey than I am is so good—healthy even. But God did not intend for me to use those people as an excuse to wait until I am older to start living the life He has called me to live. Rather, He intended to use that example to inspire and sharpen me to be who He has called me to be *today*.

The time of His favor is right now. From the very beginning, God called us personally and anointed us to let our lights shine (Matthew 5:16).

How has your age affected what you believe you can or cannot do for the Kingdom of God?

My age has affected me to not be able to participate in mission trips until later (also my brother's age too).

God has blessed each of us with purposeful and original gifts. He doesn't want to waste time and only use us when we're teenagers, high-school graduates, married, or retired. Just think! God called David to defeat Goliath and had Samuel anoint him as the future king of Israel when he was just a young shepherd boy. He said of David, "The Lord does not look at the things people look at. People look at the outward appearance, but the Lord looks at the heart" (1 Samuel 16:7). Esther was a young girl when God called her to be a vessel of His mighty glory and to save His people as the queen. Mary was a teenager when God anointed her to be the mother of Jesus Christ Himself. The King of kings doesn't see our age as a limiting factor but, rather, a shining force for His name's sake.

As I pray and let God empower me to write and speak for His glory, it would be easy to receive the lie from the enemy that I cannot possibly do these things because I'm just a teenager. I could so easily believe the lie that I need to wait until I am older so that I have more wisdom. But the King of kings comes in with truth. His Word reminds me that He has made me for such a time as this (Esther 4:14) and that in Him I have everything I could ever need.

In 2 Peter 1:3 we are told that "His divine power has given us everything we need for a godly life." This is why it

GOD made me to be a LIGHT for HIS glory today.

is so important to know who we are in God, to spend time in His Word daily. When we know the truth in and out, no matter how or when deceit slithers in, we can quickly and with a sober mind reject and rebuke and replace lies with truth in the victorious name of Jesus. The Lord doesn't need someone of a certain age, a certain degree, a certain past, or a certain platform on social media. God is simply looking for a heart that is willing to be obedient.

When does God say that you can begin to live wholeheartedly for Him? What are some ways you can be obedient right now?

God says that I can start living for Him wholeheartedly today. Some ways I can be obedient now is to volunteer (to share God's love), and not be afraid to read the bible out in public and study His word.

God's Word equips us for every good work (2 Timothy 3:17), including rebuking the lie of needing to be a certain age to make a difference. The Lord declares, "Don't let anyone look down on you because you are young, but set an example for the believers in speech, in conduct, in love, in faith and in purity" (1 Timothy 4:12). We are called to set an example of serving God, no matter how old we are.

God sees the heart that is simply willing to be whole-hearted in walking with Him. Today is the day that the Lord has made (Psalm 118:24), and we can make a difference. We can change the world. We can go everywhere and tell everyone the Good News, online and in person. We can succeed and be prosperous. What the world sees as a weakness God sees as an opportunity to show His perfect strength.

God wants to use us. We are atmosphere beautifiers, hope bringers, light radiators, and love messengers. As we abide in Jesus and He abides in us (John 15), we will lack no good thing (Psalm 34:10). The right time to do the right thing is right now.

What are you going to do today to set an example of God's heart?

For now, I will find volunteer opportunities to work at the hospital or job shadow, and look through my church's missionary option to discuss to my family about signing up. I will also continue to show God's love everyday with random acts of kindness.

DEAR GOD, THANK YOU SO MUCH FOR MAKING ME FOR SUCH A TIME AS THIS. HELP ME TO NOT BE DECEIVED THAT MY AGE IS A LIMITATION TO WHAT YOU CAN DO IN AND THROUGH ME RIGHT NOW. HELP ME TO LIVE IN LOVE WITH YOU AND YOUR WORD RIGHT NOW INSTEAD OF WAITING UNTIL I AM A CERTAIN AGE.

Sometimes WE don't realize how DARK it is until the LIGHT is turned ON.

TURN THE LIGHTS ON

You are the light of the world.
A town built on a hill cannot be hidden.

MATTHEW 5:14

Satan, the Liar

I was sitting with some of my friends in the dim cafeteria, enjoying some cookies. All of a sudden, the lights brightened, and the whole room lit up. I was able to see my friends more clearly. They are all so unique and lovely, and once the lights were turned on, I saw their beauty in a way that I couldn't see it in the dark. The yellows and reds and greens—all of the colors of the room appeared more vibrant. I was refreshed simply because I could see better. I noticed that sometimes we don't realize how dark it is until the light is turned on.

We live in a world that is ruled by the enemy. In 2 Corinthians 11:14 we are told that Satan masquerades as an angel of light. To masquerade is to pretend to be something one is not, and Satan is really good at it.

When the enemy approached Eve in the Garden of Eden

in Genesis 3, the first words out of his mouth were a question: *"Did God really say . . ."* (verse 1, emphasis added). Eve proceeded to respond with confidence in what God had told her, but with strategic determination the enemy came back with a statement that twisted the words God had spoken to her. She then began to doubt and believed the lie of the enemy, and it caused her to hide from God.

In other words, Satan is actually the father of lies who has come to steal, to kill, and to destroy (John 8:44; 10:10). He is the one who prowls around like a roaring lion, seeking whom he may devour, and God's Word tells us that he is, in fact, our enemy (1 Peter 5:8), but his appearance may deceive us (2 Corinthians 11:14-15). He is very good at making a dim room appear perfectly fine so that we may never experience the joy and freedom of what it really looks like to live with the lights turned on.

What dimness do you see around you or within you that God wants to brighten? What lies of Satan have you been listening to?

I see Satan hiding me in the
dark, preventing me from
speaking out God's words,
as well as preventing

me from loving myself, and from seeing as the beautiful woman God created me to be. Satan makes me compare myself to others, knowing full well of my weakness of being a perfectionist

The Truth Sets Us Free

The strategy of the enemy is still the same today as it was in the beginning. He questions the truth of God and feeds us lies with the purpose of leading us to walk in darkness and hide from the very One we were made to worship and be in an intimate relationship with. He seeks to blind us to who we are in Christ and who Christ really is. When it comes time to look in the mirror, instead of it being a time to praise God for the work of art that He handcrafted, it has become a time to pick apart every flaw and to despise the very things that the Lord is enthralled by.

How can we fight back against Satan's lies? When we know the truth, the truth will set us free, and we will begin to discover what life was really designed to be (John 8:32). We are told that God has called us out of the darkness and into His marvelous light (1 Peter 2:9). We were made to be children of the light (Ephesians 5:8). His light shines in the darkness and the darkness cannot overcome it (John 1:5). When we look to God, our faces are radiant, we are never covered with shame, and we never have to hide (Psalm 34:5).

You don't have to stay in darkness. You don't have to believe what Satan says, but instead, you can walk in the truth of what God says.

What are some truths about who God says you are that you can use to fight the enemy's lies?

God says I am never alone, that I am perfect, amazing, and beautiful. God will never leave my side when fighting my battle against the devil.

There are many living in this world who have listened to the lies of the enemy for so long that, just like me in that dark cafeteria, they think the dimness is normal. The enemy has blinded the minds of unbelievers so that they may not see the light of the gospel (2 Corinthians 4:4). But the light of the gospel is alive and well within every believer.

Since we are sons and daughters of the Father of Light, Jesus has told us, "You are the light of the world. A town built on a hill cannot be hidden. Neither do people light a lamp and put it under a bowl. Instead, they put it on its stand, and it gives light to everyone in the house. In the same way, let your light shine before others, that they may see your good deeds and glorify your Father in heaven" (Matthew 5:14-16).

You were meant to be a light—to drive out the darkness of Satan! God is light, and in Him there is no darkness at all (1 John 1:5). He shines in the darkness, and the darkness cannot, has not, and never will overcome Him (John 1:5). Through Jesus, we have been given the complete authority to walk in this power (Luke 10:19). God has called us out of the darkness and into His marvelous light (1 Peter 2:9), but this is not so that we may keep it to ourselves; it's so that we may share it with the world that is hurting in the darkness. We are the light of the world. Just as I was able to see the beauty of my friends and see the vibrancy of all the colors in the cafeteria once the light was turned on, so it is that when we choose to let the light of Jesus shine from within us, the beauty in others and the colors of this world will be brought to life and will be seen for what God intended in the very beginning.

What does it look like to let your light shine? In what ways do you believe God is wanting to use you to turn the lights on around you?

It feels like the whole room is lit up, and my heart flutters with happiness. He gives me opportunities to turn on the lights by sharing with others who God is, for those that don't know — him.

DEAR GOD. YOU ARE LIGHT. AND YOU SHINE
IN THE DARKNESS. AND THE DARKNESS HAS NOT OVERCOME
YOU. HELP ME TO WALK IN THE LIGHT AND TO LET MY LIGHT
SHINE BEFORE OTHERS SO THAT THEY MAY SEE MY GOOD
WORKS AND GLORIFY YOU IN HEAVEN.

MADE IN HIS IMAGE

God created mankind in his own image,
in the image of God he created them;
male and female he created them.

GENESIS 1:27

1/20/22

It's All Good

I remember in middle school I would go into my room and stare at myself in the mirror. Sometimes when I did this, I would have told you that what I saw did not look good as I nitpicked myself apart. I thought I needed to be skinnier in order to be pretty enough. Sometimes my words to myself were not kind, and I was so critical of the features I had.

But what does God's Word tell us? "In the beginning God created the heavens and the earth" (Genesis 1:1). He spoke light into existence and separated the light from the darkness. He separated the sky from the waters and the seas from the land. Then He created all of the broccoli and kale and apple trees and blueberry bushes, and He placed the sun and moon and stars so strategically in the sky. He created the birds and fish and animals and livestock and creatures moving along the ground.

And He saw that all of it was good. You and I included.

Can you think of a time when you doubted that God made you good?

The last time I doubted God made me good (around a week to 3 weeks ago) when I got overwhelmed from all the stress on me that I started to badly critcize myself, saying that I'm not good enough and that I'm dumb and stupid.

When God said that what He created was "good," He meant that it was beautiful, bountiful, and lacking no good thing. All of creation is so intricate. When I think about it, I smile so big. For example, the animals that He made reveal His creativity and humor and glory all at the same time. I love how pigeons walk. When I went to New York with my family, my mom and I laughed so hard as we imitated the fun way that pigeons bop their heads with every step that they take. Hummingbirds flap their wings about eighty times a second and eat half their weight in nectar and insects each day. God showed the bees how to produce pollen, and it does not even seem to make sense for bumblebees to be able to fly because of the size of their wings and the weight of their little bodies. But because of how God designed them, they fly. He taught the fish how to swim, and there are still so many creatures in the ocean that we have yet to learn about. He is the One who leads the baby sea turtles from the sand to the sea.

I love how He paints the skies with different strokes of yellows and hot pinks and blues for the sunrises and sunsets. My heart gets giddy simply thinking about how the clouds and sun explode in joy to praise the Lord through colors that make my jaw drop. He calls each star by name (Psalm 147:4) and has positioned the sun exactly where it

BELIEVE *that* you ARE *who* HE *says* you ARE.

needs to be to provide warmth for the earth! "The earth is the LORD's, and everything in it" (Psalm 24:1).

What is a fun fact about how God created the earth that makes you smile? How has He made your body and mind intricately?

A fun fact that makes me
smile is how God created
Ginger to try digging into my
bedsheets and roll around,
grunting in happiness (or
annoyance, because she can't
get that one itchy spot on her
back). He made my body my
own (unique & just for me).

In His Image

In all of this beauty, God said that what He created was good, but there was only one thing that He made and said was good that was in His image: human beings. In the image of God, He made male and female. In His image, He made you and me. We look at the mountains and the canyons and the seas and the landscapes and the sunshine and the stars, and we are in awe, but the Lord is enthralled by your beauty, and it is you who He delights in calling His own. You are even more creatively made, perfectly designed, and excitedly crafted than all of creation because you are made in God's image. We are the only part of His creation that was made to be in relationship with Him, and He reveals His very being by how we were purposefully made.

I once heard that insecurity is having a high view of everyone but having a low view of yourself, and arrogance is having a high view of yourself but having a low view of everyone else. Confidence, though, is having a high view of yourself and others. To walk in confidence is to know that your image and the image of every person you encounter is a reflection of the Creator. Psalm 45:11 says that "the King is enthralled by your beauty; honor Him for He is your Lord." Do you believe that? The voice of the enemy brings anxiety and either insecurity or arrogance. But God's voice brings peace and confidence, declaring that you are sealed in His identity and are an image bearer of Him.

One of the greatest ways to honor the One who made you and is enthralled by your beauty is to believe that you are who He says you are. And if we believe that we and those around us are who He says we are, then we should treat both ourselves and them as such.

How do you respond to hearing that you are made in God's image? Would you say you are mainly walking in insecurity, arrogance, or confidence? And why do you say so?

1) It makes me feel so loved, and so happy that God is always with me because I'm made in his image!

2) I would say I'm mainly walking in insecurity because I feel like I don't to call myself worthy of love and being happy of myself.

DEAR GOD, YOU ARE SO GOOD. THANK YOU FOR MAKING ME IN YOUR IMAGE AND CLAIMING ME TO BE BEAUTIFUL, BOUNTIFUL, AND LACKING NO GOOD THING. PLEASE SEARCH ME AND KNOW ME AND REVEAL ANY INSECURITY OR ARROGANCE IN ME AND REPLACE IT WITH THE CONFIDENCE OF WHO I AM IN YOU. CONFIDENCE CAN ONLY BE FOUND IN YOU.

Choose to WALK in faith & TRUST that His GRACE is SUFFICIENT.

DON'T GROW WEARY

Let us not become weary in doing good,
for at the proper time we will reap a harvest
if we do not give up.

GALATIANS 6:9

Weary but Willing

Driving home from school one day, I was so excited to rest. It had been a long day and I was mentally tired, but being out of shampoo and conditioner, I needed to go to the grocery store. In spite of my tiredness, I began to pray in faith for God to use me however He wanted to in the grocery store. I walked into the shampoo and conditioner aisle, and there was a lovely woman whom I had never had the joy of seeing before. God told me to tell her how beautiful she was, and so I looked up and said, "Excuse me, ma'am, you are so beautiful." She looked straight at me and said, "Are you serious?" I said, "Yes, ma'am, you are stunning." Before I knew it, she began to tell me personal parts of her story. Tears filled her eyes as she told me that she didn't think she was beautiful and that she had not experienced joy in a very long time and was overwhelmed with loneliness. I asked her if I could pray for her, and she said yes. In the middle of the shampoo and conditioner aisle, we boldly approached God's throne of grace. When we were done, we gave each other a hug, and she smiled.

In moments like these, as our flesh seems to be validly screaming and reminding us of how tired we are, we are given the opportunity to either obey our flesh or obey the voice of the Lord. When we choose to walk in faith and trust that His grace is sufficient to give us strength (2 Corinthians 12:9) on the days when we don't necessarily feel like it or on the days when our fuel is running low, we will experience Him doing exceedingly and abundantly greater things than what we could ever "ask or imagine, according to His power that is at work within us" (Ephesians 3:20). Through our obedience, those who are discouraged become encouraged in truth.

In what ways have you found yourself growing weary lately?

I have been mentally & physically exhausted from school, and trying to keep up with it.

_____

_____

_____

_____

_____

Jesus' Example

In Galatians 6:9, Paul spurs us on to not grow weary of doing good, for indeed we will reap a harvest in the proper time if we do not give up. The Lord is encouraging us through Paul because there are definitely moments when it is easy to grow weary of doing good. There will be days that we simply want to go and get our shampoo and conditioner and go home. Done and done, the box is checked off, and it is time for a nap. But to be a follower of Jesus means to live as Jesus lived.

Jesus sometimes had very valid reasons to ignore the people around Him and focus on Himself. In Matthew 14:13 He had just heard about the death of His cousin John the Baptist. He needed to go to a solitary place to be alone with God and process the hurt in His heart, but a large crowd of people began to follow Him. The Word says that when He saw them, He had compassion on them and healed their sick and fed all of them with only five loaves of bread and two fish.

Jesus empathizes with us in our weaknesses. Even if it is something as simple as being tired after a long day and just wanting to go in and out of the grocery store, He understands. And because He understands, we can boldly approach His throne of grace and ask for help in our time of weakness and tiredness and lack of energy (Hebrews 4:16). To be a follower of Him means to deny ourselves (Matthew 16:24) and, by His grace, have compassion on those around us regardless of how we feel.

How does the example of Jesus encourage you? Can you remember a time when God supported you through your weariness?

1) The example of Jesus encourages me to pray that no matter how tired & weary I am, Jesus can help lift that weariness

2) God is actually supporting me now at camp, where

I have the weekend to rest, have fun, and be surrounded by so many amazing people.

Called to Encourage

Just like Jesus, we have crowds of people around us, and because of the authority that we have in Christ, we can be a vessel of healing and life to them. He has called you to pray over the students in your school. He has called you to sit with the lonely at lunch. He has called you to step outside of your comfort zone and speak life into people regardless of the response. You cannot determine how others react, but you can choose to obey Jesus' call. Not tomorrow, for we are not promised tomorrow (James 4:13-14), but today because today is the day that the Lord has made so that you may rejoice and be glad in it (Psalm 118:24). He made this day for you to leave people better than how you found them.

Let us not grow weary of doing good. In the time that our flesh is weak, we can continue to run the race that has been set before us with endurance because Jesus endured the cross knowing the joy that was set before Him (Hebrews 12:1-2). People are too important to God for us to grow weary.

How can you practically make the most of every opportunity to encourage others?

Just listen to the Lord. He will tell you when to make the most of every opportunity at the right place, and time. Just pray for God's help to be a light and listen to what he has to say (and follow it!).

DEAR GOD, THANK YOU SO MUCH FOR YOUR GRACE THAT IS SUFFICIENT AND FOR YOUR STRENGTH THAT IS MADE PERFECT IN MY WEAKNESS. HELP ME TO NOT GROW WEARY OF DOING GOOD AND HELP ME TO FULLY SUBMIT TO YOU IN COMPLETE TRUST THAT YOU ARE GIVING ME THE ENDURANCE TO RUN THE RACE YOU HAVE SET BEFORE ME.

FULLY ACCEPTED

*Am I now trying to win the approval of human beings,
or of God? Or am I trying to please people? If I were still
trying to please people, I would not be
a servant of Christ.*

GALATIANS 1:10

1/23/22

Already Paid

I was in my college dorm doing some laundry, and I was so excited because doing laundry means that I get to see people and enjoy the process of getting clean clothes. I walked into the laundry room and began to switch over my load to the dryer when a young fella told me not to worry about paying. I told him thank you, but I did not fully understand what he meant.

You may know that once the load in the washer or dryer is paid for, all you need to do is press START. But because I did not understand that the kind fella had already paid for me, I spent I don't even know how long trying to pay for my load to dry. Once I realized what he had done, I began to laugh at the amount of time I had spent trying to find and do something that had already been done for me.

Jesus has already paid the price for our approval—by dying on the cross and defeating death by rising again. Through Him we are sealed in acceptance (Ephesians 1:13), yet because so many of us do not understand what He has done, we are searching for approval for I don't know how long, in places where we will never find it. In reality, our only job is to accept this gift of approval and simply START walking in the joy and freedom of it.

Where have you been seeking approval? What does it mean to you that you have God's approval through Christ?

I have been comparing myself, and been especially seeking approval of my grades, looks, and talent in whatever sport I play.

We all love to be noticed. We love to be liked. We love to be accepted and to be approved. And this isn't a bad thing, but it can quickly become dangerous when we seek to satisfy this longing with something other than God.

The decisions that we make will be based on what other people think if we are not walking in the truth that our approval is found in God alone. In Galatians 1:10, Paul says, "Am I trying to please people? If I were still trying to please people, I would not be a servant of Christ." I cannot please Christ while trying to pay for something that He already paid for. I cannot please Christ while seeking the very approval that He has already given me from a world that offers it but can never come through. Seeking our approval from the world turns into us trying to please the world, and we simply cannot fear both God and people (Proverbs 29:25).

He is worthy of all of our praise and attention (Psalm 145:3). We were made to rely on His faithfulness, and that is why it is so exhausting trying to figure out how to get approval from the world—we were not made to get our approval there. "Where [our] treasure is, there [our hearts] will be also" (Matthew 6:21). When we come to the realization that our approval isn't found in others, hope is not lost but found, and we can START walking in this hope and laughing in joy.

You are
ALREADY
fully
ACCEPTED
through
CHRIST.

Can you think of a time when you tried to please people instead of God?

> I tried by working my butt off to do schoolwork, like I been all this week before camp. I have also been working more partly so then I can look good.

An Everlasting Love

You are already fully accepted through Christ. God calls you by name and sees you for who He made you to be (Isaiah 43:1; Psalm 139:13-16), not who the world has claimed you to be. God named you before the world ever had an opportunity to speak over you. God loves you. You are His treasure. Even when you fail Him, He responds with the love that dances from His heart and says, "I have loved you with an everlasting love; I have drawn you with unfailing kindness" (Jeremiah 31:3), and nothing in all of creation can separate you from His love (Romans 8:39).

Just as I was trying to figure out how to pay for my laundry but couldn't because it had already been done, so we will remain anxious and confused until we believe that Christ is the only One who can satisfy us. In Psalm 23:1, we see that the Lord is our Shepherd and that in Him we lack nothing. In Psalm 103:5, we see that it is the Lord who satisfies our desires with good things. The Lord intentionally made us with a longing to be wanted and to be approved, but because He made it, He is the only One who can meet this need.

How does knowing you are already accepted change the way that you interact with the world around you?

I think that makes me feel more confident, stronger, and more fulfilled by God (and happier), and I can feel like I can walk tall with my head held high.

_____

_____

_____

_____

_____

_____

_____

_____

_____

_____

DEAR GOD, YOU ARE ABSOLUTELY WONDERFUL,
AND YOUR LOVE FOR ME BLOWS MY MIND. THANK YOU
FOR FULLY ACCEPTING ME. TEACH ME HOW TO RECEIVE YOUR
LOVE AND ACCEPTANCE OF ME SO THAT I MAY WALK
IN IT AND SHARE IT WITH OTHERS.

GOD works
differently
than we
MIGHT.

HERE COMES
THAT DREAMER

*Joseph went after his brothers and
found them near Dothan. But they saw him
in the distance, and before he reached them, they
plotted to kill him. "Here comes that dreamer!"
they said to each other.*

GENESIS 37:17-19

2/26/22

A Big Dream

Have you ever had a dream that caused you to wake up
laughing out loud? I once was dreaming that I was brushing
my teeth. In my dream, I went to spit the toothpaste back
into the sink, but in real life while I was sleeping I actually
spit on myself. I woke up with spit on me and laughed at
myself. It has been a handful of years, and I still find myself
cracking up about it.

But then there are other dreams that God will put on
our hearts that go beyond the joy of spitting toothpaste.

The summer before my junior year of high school, God put it on my heart to write a book. I had no idea where to begin or how it would take place or what the time frame would even vaguely look like, but with expectant confidence, I said yes and trusted that He would have His way. With a heart that was open to whatever God wanted to do, I found myself giddy and at peace even while having no idea what it was going to look like.

In Proverbs 3:5-6, we are commanded to trust in the Lord with all of our hearts and not lean on our own understanding, but in all of our ways we are told to submit to Him and He will make our paths straight. I adore how the Word of God interprets His own words because then in Philippians 4:6-7, He speaks through Paul and says, "Do not be anxious about anything, but in everything by prayer and supplication with thanksgiving let your requests be made known to God. And the peace of God, which surpasses all understanding, will guard your hearts and your minds in Christ Jesus" (ESV). In order to have peace that surpasses all understanding, we must trust in the Lord and not lean on our own understanding. So when He puts dreams on our hearts and is leading us into waters that look unfamiliar, we can have peace when we still choose to trust.

What dreams are on your heart that God may be placing there?

I've had dreams where I was laughing with my friends, and making more memories with my family (in my dreams, of course). I also had dreams about me in college or working in my potential career (nursing).

Pushback

When God gave Joseph a dream in Genesis 37, Joseph went and told his brothers about it, but they mocked him because of the things that he told them were going to happen. When God calls us to do something, it is not going to be something the world agrees with; it is going to be uncomfortable, and the steps that will be required for the dream to come to fruition are not necessarily ones that we would choose if given the opportunity.

God works differently than we might. He chose to feed five thousand men plus women and children with five loaves of bread and two fish. He chose a shepherd boy to become the king of Israel. He chose to split the Red Sea through Moses lifting his staff in the air. He chose to heal a blind man by putting mud made with spit on his eyes. He chose to send the Savior of the world in the form of a baby. His ways are higher than our ways and His thoughts are higher than our thoughts (Isaiah 55:8-9), and He knows exactly what He is doing. Therefore, when we say yes to Him, the world will make fun, the world will be confused, and the world will reject. But what if, when you walked into a room, others said, "Here comes that dreamer"—just as they did about Joseph? It would be so beautiful to be known for dreaming from the heart of God and getting excited about what He is excited about, trusting that none of His plans can be thwarted.

Where have you faced pushback against the dreams God has given you? How have you responded?

I have; I would
doubt that I could
make my Godly dreams
come true or be

afraid to try to make them
real because I would be
worried about what the
world thinks. To be honest,
I haven't done a good
enough job on pushing back
against the dark, but I will
turn to God and pray for
strength and confidence through
my actions.

Childlike Faith

There is a reason that God calls us to have childlike faith
(Matthew 18:2-4). It seems that the older we get, the less
real our dreams become. Sometimes instead of having expectant faith that nothing is impossible with God, we fade into
simply hoping it will happen or ignoring it because we are
scared of what the response from others will be.

But we are made in the image of the Ultimate Dreamer
who does not intend for those dreams to stay dreams but
to become reality. It took many years, but Joseph's dreams
came true. Because God dreams, we are called to dream,
and because His promises are faithful and true, we can trust

that they were not meant to stay in between our ears and that they will happen in His perfect time. But to Him who is able to do exceedingly and abundantly greater things than what we could ever ask or imagine, according to His power at work within us, to Him be the glory (Ephesians 3:20-21). It brings Him glory when we walk in faith.

What if, like a child, you began to dream big because you sought the dreams of God? Before time began, God had dreams specifically designed for you, and He so passionately wants to bring these dreams to reality in your life. He has chosen you as royalty in His Kingdom. May others say, "Here comes that dreamer," when they see you because your life reflects the impossible-to-possible faith that is found in the Father who promises all things to work together for you who love Him and are called according to His purpose (Romans 8:28).

Knowing that God has big dreams for your life, what does that tell you about His heart for you? How can you encourage people today in the truth that God has big dreams for them, too?

It tells me that he will use me in powerful ways, because he knows that I'm strong and

capable enough through Him
(and because he loves me!).
I can pray with them, and
maybe help push them in the
direction (if God puts me
there) of God's big plans for
them. I can also set an
example of fulfilling God's
plans by taking action of
mine.

DEAR GOD, THANK YOU FOR HAVING EXCEEDINGLY
AND ABUNDANTLY GREATER DREAMS FOR MY LIFE THAN
WHAT I COULD EVER ASK OR IMAGINE. AS I DELIGHT MYSELF
IN YOU, I ASK THAT YOU PLEASE PLACE YOUR DREAMS ON MY
HEART AND DEEPEN MY FAITH TO BELIEVE THAT
NOTHING IS IMPOSSIBLE FOR YOU. PLEASE
RESTORE MY CHILDLIKE FAITH.

Because of
YOUR courage
in CHRIST,
people will
experience
the flavor
of WHOLENESS
& FREEDOM.

TAKE NOTE

*When they saw the courage of Peter and John and
realized that they were unschooled, ordinary men, they
were astonished and they took note that these
men had been with Jesus.*

ACTS 4:13

Smell Like Jesus

My dad is such a good cook, and he cooks all the time.
Sometimes he grills in our outdoor kitchen. When he
comes back inside with food that makes our mouths water,
he smells like smoke—simply because he has been standing outside with the grill. Going to give him a hug, I smell
the smoky scent on his shirt and in his beard, and I know
where he has been.

Sometimes God will put a message on my heart to
share via social media. As this has happened over time and
I have shared in faith, I have received a variety of responses.
Some responses have been from atheists simply declaring

something along the lines of, "I don't even believe in God, but there is something about this girl that I love and that makes me smile." Getting to read comments like this makes my heart grin so wide because these precious people may not realize it yet, but the "something" that they love is Jesus. The light that we shine as we are obedient to Christ is what makes others, including nonbelievers, take note that something is different.

I once heard a quote that said, "God isn't asking for your ability; He is asking for your availability." He is not limited by what you see as limits; He just simply needs you to be willing. You don't have to look a certain way or have a certain history for God to use you. People will take note that you have been with Jesus because of your courage to love as Jesus loved. People will take note that you have been with Him because you will begin to act and smell like Him.

What smell are you carrying with you, and what do people take note of when they see your life? How has the time you've spent with Jesus affected your "smell"?

I think I kinda leave a sorta "sweet" scent, if you were to ask the people closet to me. The time

I spent with Jesus overtime has made my scent much more stronger and sweeter! (At least I can imagine.)

The Salt of the Earth

Jesus calls us "the salt of the earth" (Matthew 5:13), which is really exciting when you think about all of the things that salt does. Salt melts ice, adds flavor, creates thirst, and preserves. These things should be true of us. When we walk in the grace and truth of Jesus, hearts of stone will melt into hearts of flesh (Ezekiel 36:26). Because of our courage in Christ, people will experience the flavor of wholeness and freedom. When I think of flavor, I think of brightness and life, and this is what Jesus offers us. He is our abundant life. When we've been walking closely with Jesus, our lives will impact those around us because He will be tasted and seen in and through us (Psalm 34:8).

Others will recognize their thirst for this abundant life because they see the living water that flows from within us.

Jesus gives living water, and whoever drinks from the water He gives will never go thirsty again (John 4:14). When we are the salt of the earth, those around us who do not know Jesus are made aware of their thirst which has not been satisfied yet—because they have not tasted the living water that only Jesus can offer. And finally, God will use us to preserve His beauty in the world and in the hearts of others.

In what ways are you being "salty" in the world?

By being kind to others, giving, trusting of others (and God), by staying consistent with praying (nightly).

God has ordained every encounter you have with another person, and He has a purpose for their life. When you choose to be His vessel, this purpose can be revealed in their life because "we are . . . Christ's ambassadors as though God were making His appeal through us" (2 Corinthians 5:20). An ambassador is a representative, so when we are told by God that we are ambassadors of Christ, He is telling us that we have been given the powerful and important role of representing Christ here on earth. How we live, how we speak, how we love—it all is a representation of Christ in us!

By our simply having the courage to be obedient in the ordinary, people will take note that we have been with Jesus because they will encounter Jesus through their encounter with us. Just as I smell the grill on my daddy when he walks in the house, others will smell the sweet fragrance of God's presence in our lives because of how we spend time with Him.

What does it say about Jesus, knowing that others take note when we have been with Him? How will others take note that you have been with Jesus today?

Others can see the
difference of their
changed heart from being

with Jesus. Others will
take note of me being
more patient, open,
warmer, and more
forgiving (and slow to
judge).

DEAR GOD, I NOTICE YOU AND ACKNOWLEDGE YOU
WITH AWE. HELP ME TO LIVE IN SUCH A WAY THAT OTHERS WILL
LOOK AT MY LIFE AND TAKE NOTE THAT I HAVE BEEN WITH
YOU. USE ME TO BE A REFLECTION OF YOU SO THAT
THROUGH ME OTHERS WILL COME TO
INTIMATELY KNOW YOU.

NO TIME FOR COMPLAINTS

5/21/22

*Do everything without grumbling or
arguing, so that you may become blameless
and pure, "children of God without fault in a warped
and crooked generation." Then you will shine
among them like stars in the sky.*

PHILIPPIANS 2:14-15

Rainy Days

It has been raining a lot where I live lately. For me, sunny days typically bring smiles while cloudy days bring an attitude drop, but recently I have found just as much joy in the cloudy and rainy days as in the sunny and clear ones because I discovered in His Word that "the clouds are the dust of His feet" (Nahum 1:3) and that He will come to us like the rain (Hosea 6:3). Isaiah 55:10-11 tells me that just "as the rain and the snow come down from heaven and do not return to it without watering the earth and making it bud and flourish," so also the Word of God that "goes out from [His] mouth . . . will not return to [Him] empty, but will accomplish . . . the purpose for which [He] sent it."

So now when it rains, I get so excited because it reminds me of the faithfulness of His Word and how He is with me. My heart rejoices in the clouds because I am comforted by the truth that He is watching over me. It is a perspective change that can only happen in Him because it is in His presence that the fullness of joy is found (Psalm 16:11). To delight in Him is to have a perspective shift. When our minds are governed by the Spirit, we have life and peace because we are delighting in His Word.

Where in your life do you see that there can be a perspective shift for the good?

Maybe shift MY perspective
to what God would do,
rather than shamefully
let my tongue speak.

Remember the Israelites? They had just been set free from being held in slavery by the Egyptians. The Lord was guiding them to the Promised Land and gave them manna from heaven and quail to eat (Exodus 16). He gave them water from a rock (Exodus 17:1-7) and led them by a pillar of fire at nighttime and a cloud at daytime (Exodus 13:21). He blessed His people with peace and gave them strength and led them out of bondage, yet they grumbled and argued because what they had was never enough for them.

But the future is never going to be better if every step you take is with an ungrateful heart of complaints. To complain is to express discontent or annoyance, but God says to "do everything without grumbling or arguing, so that you may become blameless and pure, 'children of God without fault in a warped and crooked generation.' Then you will shine among them like stars in the sky as you hold firmly to the word of life" (Philippians 2:14-16). God calls us to a higher standard.

We all have storms that we go through. We have cloudy seasons and rainy circumstances, and in these times we have every reason to grumble and argue, but there is power in choosing to abide in the promises of God. His Word says that He is working all things together for the good of those who love Him and are called according to His

Dancing with JESUS does not look like STEPPING in a straight LINE.

purpose (Romans 8:28). So when we see something that does not look good, we can choose to trust God. Usually, the moments of our lives where it makes the most sense to complain are the very moments in which the Lord is longing to reveal to us the deepest joy.

What does it mean to do everything without grumbling or complaining? In what ways or circumstances do you notice that you are quick to complain?

Meaning you have to turn to God and pray for a still heart, and keep being a light of his by being grateful and patient of what God has done for me. One example which I am quick to complain on is other peoples' driving styles, and my school, on how they present themselves.

I had always looked at Paul's words in Philippians 2 through the lens of not complaining or arguing about the things going on around me, but never did I think about not complaining or arguing about the things going on within me. When my weaknesses are brought to the front and center of my mind, and the things I don't do well are a focus, I sometimes find myself grumbling and complaining about how weak and unable I am. And each time I speak negatively over myself, I fuel the flame of the evil one so that he would have all the more encouragement to attack with his arrows of deceit.

God calls us to speak His Word over ourselves just as much as He calls us to speak life and truth over others and the things happening around us. May our hearts not only be pure in how we see others but also in how we see ourselves. Instead of complaining about where we are personally in our walk with Him, may we be thankful that we have room to grow and that we get to navigate through the riches of God's grace. It is such a beautiful dance. Some days I take three steps forward. Some days I take two steps back. Some days I take a step to the side, but hey, it's growth. Dancing with Jesus does not look like stepping in a straight line. It is full of steps forward and backward and sideways. It is led by Him and is something so beautiful that we do not have time for complaints.

The beauty of giving your life to Christ is that you don't respond as the world does. You can be a shining star bringing light to everyone around you. God's will for us is to "rejoice always, pray continually, give thanks in all circumstances" (1 Thessalonians 5:16-18). He doesn't say to rejoice when it is easy but all of the time, and by doing so you will not only be satisfied in Him, but you will also bring the satisfaction that only comes from Jesus to the darkness around you.

What are some truths you can speak over your own life? How can you intentionally be grateful today?

God has a plan bigger than your own imagination can even think of, and he will be there every step of the way. So, resist the devil, and forever be grateful for God never leaving your side. Pray everyday to thank him and to never leave his.

Be the light that God
called you to be.

DEAR GOD, THANK YOU FOR LONGING TO GIVE
ME JOY. HELP ME TO CHOOSE GRATITUDE EVEN WHEN MY
CIRCUMSTANCES GIVE ME REASON TO COMPLAIN.

TO SEE AS HE SEES

*The Lord said to Samuel, "Do not consider his
appearance or his height. . . . The Lord does not look at
the things people look at. People look at the outward
appearance, but the Lord looks at the heart."*

1 SAMUEL 16:7

5/25/22

Outward Beauty

I had the blessing of getting to be the homecoming queen
of my high school, which meant that the following year I
got to come back and pass on the crown to the next queen.
Standing on the football field and seeing all of the beautiful
girls in their dresses, I went to hug them and tell them how
gorgeous they looked and how sweet it was to see them. The
time came for their dads to escort them down the field, and
I stood at the opposite end as giddy as could be. With my
overalls on, fancy shoes fitted in readiness, and the crown
in my hands, I waited for the next queen to be announced.

After all of the homecoming maids had been escorted
down the field, the announcer was suspenseful in every
word leading up to the name of the queen. We all waited

excitedly, and as he spoke the name of the next queen, my heart burst in celebration. The queen was my next-door neighbor. She was so precious, and I couldn't get to her fast enough—I started dancing on my way to her and embraced her. As I placed the crown on her head, all my heart could find to say was, "You are so beautiful. I love you." Tears filled her eyes, and she was overwhelmed with gratitude and awe.

Some of us have been homecoming queen and some of us haven't, but I do know that we have all felt insecure at times, and this feeling captured our attention as though it was all that mattered. We have all felt like we are not pretty enough or do not measure up in how we look, but God looks at the heart. He does not make mistakes, but He makes masterpieces, and He declares each of us His original and beautiful masterpiece (Ephesians 2:10).

In what ways do you look at the outward appearance of others, or even yourself, instead of the heart?

I look at myself whenever I'm feeling vulnerable, like when I see myself in the mirror or when the spotlight is on me when someone tries to compliment me. I then judge myself on how pretty everyone else looks and how I fail to even compare to them.

Beautiful to God

Leading up to this point, I had been specifically asking God to help me see myself through His eyes and to also see others the way that He sees them. God loves when we come to Him, and He loves to give us a Spirit of wisdom and revelation so that we may know Him better. When I placed the crown on the homecoming queen's head, the Lord whispered into my heart that this is how He sees you and me. He calls us by name unashamedly and with great assurance and is ecstatic to be with us because He loves us so much that He begins dancing over us—He simply cannot contain His joy. Rejoicing over us with loud singing (Zephaniah 3:17) and quieting our hearts with His love, He speaks, "You are so beautiful. I love you," and "He crowns [us] with love and compassion" (Psalm 103:4). We are His treasures.

Let US be
EAGER to
speak LIFE
over one
ANOTHER.

1 Samuel 16:7 tells us, "The Lord does not look at the things people look at. People look at the outward appearance, but the LORD looks at the heart," and regardless of where we are, God is our mighty Warrior who saves and has invited us to be His sons and daughters in His Kingdom. There is nothing in the past or present or future that separates us from the love of God that is in Christ Jesus our Lord (Romans 8:38-39). He chose us before time began (Ephesians 1:4) and proclaimed that we are each His masterpiece.

What does it say about the Lord when we see that He looks at the heart rather than the outward appearance?

He looks at how loving, kind, caring, strong we are to others. It also means He looks at how much weight He puts on our hearts, which is heavy in love and light in peace and joy. He looks at our sweet personality, not on our attractive looks.

It was incredible that the precious soul I had the delight of crowning was my actual next-door neighbor because Jesus has commanded us to love our neighbor as ourselves. Just as I was dancing to crown my next-door neighbor, God calls us to love our neighbor as He loves. Because God does not look at the outward appearance but at the heart, we are then called to love people regardless of what they look like. When we know who we are in Christ, we are compelled by His love to dance to other people, eager to let them know who they are in the Father. We have been called by name to crown our neighbors in the truth that God has called them by name, that they are so beautiful to Him, and that He loves them, too. Every person we meet is our neighbor; therefore, let us be eager to speak life over one another just as our Heavenly Father has done for us.

What person do you need to start seeing the way that God sees? How can you speak life over them?

I need to start seeing the way God sees those who I personally believe are annoying (such as some of the kids in my tennis class) and those who are misguided away from the Word (such as my relatives, etc.). I can speak life to them by showing love to them and to everyone else (not just those that need it). those that in God's eyes he sees as beautiful.

DEAR GOD, THANK YOU SO MUCH FOR CALLING ME BY NAME AND FOR SEEING ME WITH EYES OF LOVE. PLEASE HELP ME TO SEE MYSELF THE WAY THAT YOU SEE ME AND TO SEE OTHERS THE WAY THAT YOU SEE THEM.

FRIENDS are treasured GIFTS who were MADE to champion ONE ANOTHER on.

CALL OUT THE FUNK

Blessed is the one who does not walk in step with the wicked or stand in the way that sinners take or sit in the company of mockers.

PSALM 1:1

5/31/22

A Loving Reminder

When I played soccer, I would come home from practice pretty sweaty and smelling quite funky, but because I had been practicing with my team for the last several hours, I was not aware of how intense the funky smell was. I would be so excited to talk about the day with my family, but not even two minutes into our conversation, my parents would interrupt me in love to tell me that I needed to go take a shower before our conversation could continue, because I did not smell good.

It is so important for us to surround ourselves with friends who will call out our funk in love (Ephesians 4:15) because they see the goodness that God is calling us to walk in, and they want us to experience all that He has for us.

Sometimes the Holy Spirit will reveal funk to us that is in our hearts by allowing us to simply witness the lives of those around us. By surrounding ourselves with people who are intentionally seeking God first, we will be encouraged to want to keep growing in intimacy with Him as well. When we unknowingly walk in funk, it affects not only us but also everyone around us, and that is why we need to have people in our lives who call us out in love.

Who do you have in your life to call out your funk? Whose funk are you calling out?

My parents, my brother (mostly them), and my friends (Isabel, Lauren, and Erika) sometimes. And I do the same for them too (plus help Simone out when I can).

Celebration Friendship

Friends in Christ are not only those who call us out in our funk, but they are those who help us walk out of it, encourage us, hold us accountable, and build us up to be the incredible world changers that God has called us to be. They pull out the radiant beams of light that God knitted within us and help us to see them for ourselves. Friends are treasured gifts who were made to champion one another.

Friendship that God intended is a celebration kind of friendship. In Christ, we delight to see one another do well, and as I was once told, we do not tolerate each other's victories, but we celebrate them. Woe to the person who falls and has no one to pick him up (Ecclesiastes 4:10). Just as iron sharpens iron, one friend sharpens another (Proverbs 27:17).

Who do you have to call out the goodness in your life? Whose goodness are you calling out?

My mom is the main person who calls out the goodness of my life (but same everyone else). I try to call out the goodness of my parents' and friends' lives *although I should do a better job supporting my brother (Ethan) move.*

Psalm 1 Friends

Growing up, our family's motto was Psalm 1:1-3. My parents constantly spoke it over our home, and my brother and I engraved it upon our hearts. It says, "Blessed is the one who does not walk in step with the wicked or stand in the way that sinners take or sit in the company of mockers, but whose delight is in the law of the LORD, and who meditates on His law, day and night. That person is like a tree planted by streams of water, which yields its fruit in season and whose leaf does not wither—whatever they do prospers." This, broken down, is simply saying that we will be blessed by choosing godly friends and daily spending time with God in His Word.

I call my friends my Psalm 1 friends. In order for us to pour into people who do not know Jesus, we must have people in our lives that are pouring into us as well. If I am not surrounding myself with Psalm 1 friends, then instead of influencing the world for God's glory, I will be influenced by the world and conform to its patterns. Bad company corrupts good morals, so my core company must be with people who build me up in His truth and walk with me in His love—then when I am in other company, I can be an influence of truth and love on them. So not only is it essential to surround ourselves with friends who will call out our funk in love, but it is also very important that we do not choose our best buds to be people who are not walking with Jesus and are choosing to walk in their own funk.

God designed friends to be those who help you become who He has called you to be, and He wants you to help them become who He has called them to be too. We were made in the image of the God of relationships, and this is why we long for relationships. By seeking Christ together in our friendships, we will be like trees that are planted by streams of water. We will yield our fruit in season and our leaves will never wither, and whatever we do will prosper.

What does it say about God when we hear that He wants us to have good friendships? What can you do to strengthen the friendships He has given you?

He wants us to have good relationships which only further deepens our relationship with Him. And he wants us to have good friendships where you can see God's work in them as well as in you. We can work together to bring out the right each of us was ——— given by God.

DEAR GOD, IT IS SO AWESOME THAT YOU ARE THE GOD OF RELATIONSHIPS AND THAT YOU HAVE MADE ME TO BE IN RELATIONSHIPS WITH OTHER PEOPLE. LEAD ME TO BUILD RELATIONSHIPS WITH PEOPLE WHO SHARPEN ME AND SPUR ME ON IN MY WALK WITH YOU. LEAD ME IN PSALM 1 FRIENDSHIPS.

ALL-INCLUSIVE

You, Lord, are a compassionate and gracious God,
slow to anger, abounding in love and faithfulness.

PSALM 86:15

7/11/22

New Every Morning

We went on a family vacation one year to Jamaica. It was so much fun, and every day around three o'clock it would begin to pour, and the Jamaicans would then get off duty from the waterslides, and they would come onto the beach, and we would play soccer in the rain. My heart was smiling bigger than my face could. The sweetest lady braided my hair one day, and there would be some days when we lay on the beach and other days when we went snorkeling. We took family pictures one evening at sunset and found starfish in the Caribbean. It was absolutely beautiful.

I have to tell you, though, that one of the best parts about this trip was that it was all-inclusive, meaning that the soft-serve ice cream was unlimited. When we woke up, we could get ice cream. When we wanted a snack, we could go get ice cream. Before we went to bed, we could go get ice cream. It was already paid for, and the amount that we could have was endless. Ice cream was always available to us.

God's mercies are like this in a sweet way. "His mercies . . . are new every morning" (Lamentations 3:22-23, ESV), and they are all-inclusive and always available to us. He gives them to us as a gift. When we wake up in the morning, His mercies are there to greet us with compassion that never fails.

What does having new mercies every morning show about God's heart toward you? What does it mean for you to personally walk in His mercies that are all-inclusive?

By walking with the Lord, I walk with His mercies guiding me and protecting me, and showing me the beautiful and comforting parts of God's creation.

Undeserved

Mercy means not receiving the punishment that we very well deserve to receive—it means we receive an undeserved pardon instead! God is compassionate and gracious. He is slow to anger, abounding in love and faithfulness (Psalm 86:15). We do not deserve this love and mercy, but in His kindness, God greets us with it from His heart every day. To sin means to miss the mark of perfection or to fall short, and according to His Word, we have all sinned and fallen short of the glory of God (Romans 3:23). This sin is worthy of death and complete separation from God because He is holy and perfect and cannot be in the presence of sin, but through the perfect sacrifice of His Son, Jesus Christ, we are rescued from the outcome of death and separation from Him.

We were not made to live in shame. Because of His mercies that are new every morning, we do not have to be consumed with the ways of this world or by desires that do not please Him. We live in a broken world, and it is easy to get wrapped up in the chaos of it. It is easy to be hindered and entangled in the distractions, but because of His mercies we can take a deep breath in Him. Rather than being hindered, let His mercies launch you forward in life and forgiveness (Hebrews 12:1-3). Instead of being entangled, let Him embrace you in His strong and compassionate arms that are upholding you and will never let you go.

GOD'S mercies are all-INCLUSIVE & always AVAILABLE to us.

What has consumed you lately—the world? Or God's mercies?
How has God shown His mercies to you?

Lately, it's been the world.
The Lord has shown His
mercies through the loving
people that I love, and
through my more frequent
reading of the Word (giving
me little bits of wisdom).

Dancing with God

Our relationship with God is the most beautiful of dances. Just as a little girl stands on her daddy's toes in the kitchen while they dance together, so we stand on the toes of our Heavenly Father and dance with Him. And just as the little girl is not dancing in her own strength but, rather, in the strength of every step her father takes, so it is that we cannot dance on our own, but our strength comes from every step taken by our Heavenly Father. We breathe in His mercies, He sweeps us off our feet, and we continue to dance in Him. We never have to fear that this strength and comfort will desert us, because His mercies never fail. They are always available to us because nothing in all of creation can separate us from the love of God (Romans 8:37-39).

If we were to trace the steps of a dance, more than likely it would not form a straight line. Some days we take three steps forward in our walk with God, the next day we may take two steps backward, and the next day may look like a step to the side. Our dance with God is not going to be a perfect and straight line, but because of His mercies, we are not consumed by the days when it feels like we are making no progress. We can know that He is upholding us every step that we take.

How can you reflect God's mercies in the lives of other people today?

By being the kind, and forgiving person that He strives for us to be. We can do little random acts of kindness, such as putting gospel stickers on people's cars. It's also good to be a shoulder to cry on for your family and friends that need it.

DEAR GOD, THANK YOU FOR YOUR MERCIES
THAT ARE BRAND NEW EVERY SINGLE MORNING! TEACH
ME HOW TO DANCE IN YOUR MERCIES TODAY AND TO EXTEND
THEM TO THOSE I GET TO ENCOUNTER.

JESUS came to CARRY my burdens for ME.

WELL RESTED

*Come to me, all you who are weary and burdened,
and I will give you rest. Take my yoke upon you and
learn from me, for I am gentle and humble in heart,
and you will find rest for your souls. For my
yoke is easy and my burden is light.*

MATTHEW 11:28-30

7/27/22

Overwhelmed

One day I called my dad, and as I began to tell him that
I was overwhelmed, tears filled my eyes. My heart was so
heavy and burdened. It was a time of my life when many
new and exciting things were happening in relationships
and traveling and projects and schoolwork. It was quite a
lot. They were all good things, but in it all, I felt like but-
ter on toast that was spread so thin. As I was sharing with
my dad what was on my heart, he lovingly made me feel
so secure as he simply sighed with me. All I could hear was
the sigh of his voice. I was quiet, just sitting with the sound
of his voice that helped me take a deep breath for a second.

He then asked me when the last time was that I sat still
with Jesus alone and did not do anything. I thought about

it, and I realized that it had been a while since I went to be alone—just me and Him and no one else. My dad said, "He wants you to." He encouraged me to go and sit in the grass and watch the butterflies and not worry about being with anyone, not worry about any deadline, not worry about anything on my phone, but to simply focus on being with the Father. He explained to me that all of the burdens in my life that I had been taking on were never mine to carry, but that Jesus came to carry them for me. He reminded me that Jesus said, "Come to me, all you who are weary and burdened, and I will give you rest. Take my yoke upon you and learn from me, for I am gentle and humble in heart, and you will find rest for your souls. For my yoke is easy and my burden is light" (Matthew 11:28-30).

Have you been overwhelmed lately? What do you see in the heart of Jesus when you read that He wants to give you rest?

I haven't been overwhelmed lately, but I have a feeling I will be with school & senior year set -up. When He wants to give us rest, He sees

how much we are hurting
from sacrificing too much
(for us to handle (overwhelmed)).
when we hurt, He hurts
too. He just wants to take
the pain away.

Renewed in Him

The next day I took action and did what my dad had suggested. I went to a quiet place alone and spent the day with Jesus. It was only us. I did not work or get on my phone, but I simply prayed and read His Word and breathed in the fresh air as the wind danced through the trees, and I colored a little bit. It was so refreshing to go away and spend alone time with Him and let Him give me rest because that is what He loves to do for us. He knows that we need it even when we don't realize that we do. This is why in Psalm 23:1-2 David writes that the Lord, who is our Shepherd, makes us "lie down in green pastures." He is the One who "leads [us] beside quiet waters." He knows what we need.

When my heart is overwhelmed, He leads me to the Rock that is higher than me, and it is only in Him that my strength can be renewed (Psalm 61:2; Isaiah 40:31).

Just as I was able to call my dad when I was overwhelmed, we were made to call upon our Heavenly Father when our hearts are overwhelmed, and in the most comforting and secure way, He will sigh over us and meet us right where we are. Jesus said that He is gentle and humble in heart and that His yoke is easy, and His burden is light. He wants to spend one-on-one time with you and me.

When and where do you go to spend time alone with Jesus? What draws you closest to Him?

I spend time with Jesus when I go on walks (seeing His beautiful creation) and when I do my own bible study (reading the Word, devotionals, etc.). I also pray one-on-one with Him too.

We cannot function in the way that each of us was designed to function if we are not making it a priority to spend time alone with the very One who made us in His image (Genesis 1:27). Looking at the life of Jesus, we see that He would be healing the sick, and then He would retreat to be alone with His Father. He would be teaching the crowds, and then He would depart from them to be alone with His Father. He danced in such a beautiful rhythm of going to a quiet place to pray, and if it was necessary for Jesus to go to the Father in solitude, then it is necessary that we routinely do that as well. Jesus lived in such a way that we should live as He did (1 John 2:6).

He wants us to come to Him and enjoy His presence. For any relationship to grow, we must spend time together—and that applies to our relationship with God as well. He wants us to come and dance with Him, and He wants to show us the flowers that He is blooming for spring, and He wants to reveal sweet treasures of His Word to us. He wants to show us priceless qualities that He knitted within us that we have yet to see. He wants to laugh with us. He wants to give us rest.

We were not made to be anxious and overwhelmed and exhausted but, rather, at peace, at rest, and restored.

How has God refreshed you lately? How can being well rested in the presence of God enable you to love others better?

God has refreshed me this summer of rest, of being able to relax at home for a little while.

Being well rested helps us clear our minds, and with God's help, our souls.

DEAR GOD, YOU ARE SO KIND TO ME. THANK YOU FOR CALLING ME OUT TO BE ALONE WITH YOU SO THAT I MAY FIND REST. TEACH ME HOW TO BE STILL IN YOU AND TO TAKE ON YOUR YOKE THAT IS EASY AND YOUR BURDEN THAT IS LIGHT.

BROKEN ZIPPERS

The thief comes only to steal and kill and destroy;
I have come that they may have life,
and have it to the full.

JOHN 10:10

Overflowing

Just want you to know, you are more than I could have ever asked for in a daughter. Your love for people and the Lord is like none I have ever seen. Thank you for being so honoring and faithful with the precious blood of Christ. With your smile, your big brown eyes, your beautiful teeth, those socks on the outside of your pants, well . . . you're a walking backpack crammed full of the gospel, love, forgiveness, and mercy of Jesus, and it is falling out of every pocket, and you've basically broken the zippers!!! You don't belong in a locker, and you don't belong in a corner, you belong on a stage! God needs you and trusts you with His most precious creation . . . people! I love you, sweet Emma Mae.

I received this text from my outstanding daddy a couple of hours before I was about to go speak at a conference, and it is definitely one of the best text messages I have ever received. It not only left me feeling so uplifted but spurred me on to uplift others, too.

Jesus came so that we may have everything in abundance, more than we expect—life in its fullness until we overflow (John 10:10)—and this is a gift that we have in relationship with Him. To be overflowing in life is to be overflowing in Jesus, and to be overflowing in Jesus is to be overflowing with the characteristics of who He is. Our zippers will be busting off from being so full of Him!

What is revealed in God's character when you see that He wants you to be crammed full, overflowing, and busting at the zippers with His life?

_____

_____

_____

_____

_____

_____

_____

_____

_____

_____

_____

All the Fruit

I love how Galatians 5:22-23 says, "The Holy Spirit produces this kind of fruit in our lives: love, joy, peace, patience, kindness, goodness, faithfulness, gentleness, *AND* self-control" (NLT, emphasis added). Not "*OR.*" God doesn't give us the instruction to pick and choose what fruit we feel like bearing, but He says that when we are living by His Spirit, this is the fruit that we will bear. We cannot experience the fullness of God if we are not willing to fully give ourselves to Him. The Lord does not settle on us; therefore, we cannot settle on ourselves. He has given us His whole Spirit, and to only see a little bit of who He is, is to miss out on all that He has for us.

We are called to be like a backpack that is crammed full, overflowing, with zippers that are breaking. This is such an exciting image of how God has called us to

To be
OVERFLOWING
in LIFE is
to be
OVERFLOWING
in JESUS.

live—overflowing with His Spirit. When we truly give our lives to Christ and pick up our cross to follow Him, the Holy Spirit does not enter our hearts partially, but He is fully there to help us and show us and live through us fully. In John 15, Jesus promises that when we remain in Him and He in us, we will bear much fruit. Therefore, it does not make sense to wake up and decide that we are going to have joy but not patience today. We wake up in the Spirit, meaning everything of the Spirit belongs to us, and we are called to walk in Him, so let us keep in step with the Spirit (Galatians 5:25).

Which fruit of the Spirit have you thought isn't for you because it is too difficult? How is God growing that fruit in you?

_____

_____

_____

_____

_____

_____

_____

_____

_____

_____

Poured Out

Of course, we do not walk in the Spirit perfectly, and there are characteristics of the Spirit that are not as easy to embrace, but this is not an excuse for us to not embrace them. If we were made in His image, imagine the abundance we will experience as we choose to walk in all that He is. If God has called you to it, it is going to be beautiful, and He will help you get there and experience the abundance of all that it is.

God looks at you and says that you are more than what He could ever ask for in a child. He chose you, and He wants you. He gave you your beautiful smile, and He gave you the lovely eyes that you have, and He came so that you may be crammed full, overflowing, busting at the zippers with His life and with the fruits of His Spirit. You were not made to be in a corner or in a locker but to be the light of the world. He has called you to the stage, and on this stage, He wants to overflow your cup (Psalm 23:5) so that you can pour into the lives of people around you that have yet to experience the power of the overflow.

How can you pour into people today who have yet to experience the power of the overflow?

_____

_____

_____

_____

_____

_____

_____

_____

_____

DEAR GOD, THANK YOU FOR THE HOLY SPIRIT.
HELP ME TO WALK BY THE HOLY SPIRIT AND LEAD ME
TO WALK IN THE EXCITING ABUNDANCE OF ALL THAT YOU ARE.
FOR I KNOW THAT WHEN I REMAIN IN YOU AND
YOU IN ME, I WILL BEAR YOUR FRUIT.

WE have
complete
CONTROL over
what WE
plant in our
THOUGHTS.

THE GARDEN OF THOUGHTS

*We demolish arguments and every pretension
that sets itself up against the knowledge of God, and
we take captive every thought to make it
obedient to Christ.*

2 CORINTHIANS 10:5

We Control What We Plant

Last summer, as a surprise, my dad planted 75 to 100 sunflowers in our backyard! I grinned every time I walked outside and saw how they would grow so tall and full and bright as they looked toward the sun. My dad's garden was such a powerful reflection of our minds. My dad purposefully planted sunflower seeds. He watered them and gave them sunlight. He didn't plant apple seeds expecting sunflowers, but he planted what he intended to grow. In the same way, we have complete control over what we plant in our thoughts.

I am the gardener of my mind. I determine what gets planted, what gets watered, and what—like weeds—gets taken out. In 2 Corinthians 10:5, the Holy Spirit speaks through Paul to let us know that we must take every thought captive and make it obedient to Christ, but I cannot take captive a thought that is disobedient if I do not know what is obedient. I cannot take a lie captive and replace it with the truth if I do not know what the truth is.

Philippians 4:8 gives us a list of flowers we should plant in our minds: the flowers of loveliness, purity, nobility, righteousness, truth, admirability, praiseworthiness, and excellence. These are the flowers that God has told us to plant in our gardens because these are the thoughts that are from Him.

God's Word has power to demolish and replace every lie. What does that show you about the authority of God's Word?

_____

_____

_____

_____

_____

_____

Uproot the Weeds

Sometimes weeds that are not from this list of flowers grow in our minds and intertwine with the beauty of the flowers, producing hindrances and crippling limitations when we allow them to take root. Our thoughts determine what we talk about, how we act, and eventually who we become. If we let the weeds of insecurity take root, then insecurity will grow. If we let the weeds of fear and doubt and worry slither in, and we do not uproot them, then our decisions will stem from bad roots.

Don't let intruders crash the joyous party of life and holiness that your mind was designed to be. Our minds were handmade with delight to be a field of wildflowers that reflect the freedom that we have in Christ and His peace that He has given us. There is power in daily spending time in God's Word because no matter how nasty and overwhelming the weeds that are trying to take over your garden may seem, you can boldly know that the same power that raised Jesus from the grave lives inside of you, and therefore, you have been given the role of planting seeds of His Word that will stand forever (Isaiah 40:8). With God's Word and His strength, you can defeat and pull those weeds and replace them with the truth that sets us free (John 8:32). You have complete control of what gets planted and what gets pulled.

What are you planting in your mind? What weeds need to be pulled?

_____

_____

_____

_____

_____

_____

_____

_____

Be Intentional

Tending the garden of our minds means being intentional about filtering our thoughts with God's truth. It means being purposeful and attentive to what movies and shows we are watching, the music we are listening to, and the people we are being influenced by. Weeds don't come in all at once, and flowers don't grow in a heartbeat. It is little by little. The more we settle and compromise in these and other areas, the more weeds will grow. But on the other hand, the more we spend time daily reading God's Word, talking with godly friends, listening to wholesome music, and watching pure movies, the more our flowers will bloom.

One practical way that I replace the weeds of my mind with God's truth is by finding three verses that combat the lie that I have let come into my garden. For example, if I am fighting the weed of fear, I will go and find three Scriptures that specifically speak on fear—this is the best weed killer. I speak these truths out loud and pray over them and write them down and believe them! I can speak His Word out loud all day long, but if I do not believe what I am speaking, then I am not walking in the power that it could have in my life.

Sunflowers are heliotropic, which means that they look more and more towards the sun as they grow until they are fully facing the sun. In the same way, the more we grow in our relationship with Jesus, the more we look to Him and radiate His glory. When we decide to step into the gardening role that we have been given with authority through Jesus, and we remain true to our list of flowers, beauty will bloom within us. Even more, it will be an overflow that inspires gardeners all around us to know that they are also bought at a high price by God, and with their thoughts, they, too, have been called to honor Him who lives inside of them. For it is no longer we who live, but Christ who lives in us (Galatians 2:20). All pesky weeds must flee in the name of Jesus.

*How do your thoughts affect your encounters with those
around you? How do you see yourself thinking differently
when you have been filling your mind with God's Word?*

_____

_____

_____

_____

_____

_____

_____

_____

DEAR GOD, THANK YOU FOR GIVING ME CONTROL
OF WHAT I THINK ABOUT. PLEASE HELP ME TO HAVE
THE MIND-SET OF JESUS AND TO THINK ABOUT WHATEVER IS
OF YOU. SHOW ME THE WEEDS IN MY MIND AND HELP
ME TO UPROOT THEM AND PLANT FLOWERS
OF YOUR WORD INSTEAD.

YOU ARE INVITED

*He chose us in him before the creation of the world
to be holy and blameless in his sight.*

EPHESIANS 1:4

A Forgotten Invitation

In my senior year of high school, I was so blessed to be crowned homecoming queen. Later in the year, one of the leaders of our school's student council came up to me and handed me an envelope that said, *"Dear Miss Homecoming Queen,"* on the front. Being with other students, I didn't want to draw attention to myself. I decided to put the letter in my backpack so that I could open it later in private. About one month went by that consisted of me thinking about opening the letter when I wasn't near my backpack and me forgetting about the letter when I had my backpack with me. I continued to forget, and I continued to put it off.

Finally, I opened up the envelope on January 1 of my

senior year, during Christmas break. As I began to read, I realized that I had been officially invited to participate in a football bowl parade and be on national TV and wear an elegant ballgown. My eyes continued to scan through the letter, and I quickly came to be informed that the event had taken place a couple of days previously. I'd missed it! So much goodness was planned and waiting for me to simply accept, and I missed it because I didn't open the envelope!

Ephesians 1:7-8 tells us that in Jesus we are purposefully invited by name to walk in "redemption through his blood . . . in accordance with the riches of God's grace that he lavished on us." God has officially invited you and me into a relationship with Him, and in this relationship with Him, we are fully invited to be all that He has called us to be, fully invited to receive every spiritual blessing in Christ.

According to Ephesians 1:1-14, what is God inviting you to?

_____

_____

_____

_____

_____

_____

_____

_____

_____

_____

An Undeserved Gift

The invitation to receive Jesus as our Lord and Savior is outstanding, and none of us is deserving of such a gift, but because of God's grace, He gives us favor that we do not deserve. We are robed in His righteousness, and our sins are made as pure as snow through Jesus (Isaiah 61:10; 1:18). The gift of spending eternity with Jesus is not where our invite ends, but we are invited to dance in freedom and victory and celebration while we are still here on earth. In 2 Peter 1:3, we are told that God's divine power has given us everything that we need for a godly life through our knowledge of Him who called us by His own glory and goodness. He doesn't give us this gift of having everything that we need to walk in His calling because we deserve it but because of His "glory and goodness." It is all about Him, and He wants us to be a part of it. We are all invited and have each been given an envelope with our name intentionally handwritten upon it.

We are
INVITED to
taste & see
the HEART of
GOD in every
aspect of our
LIVES.

Have you accepted God's gift of grace? Did you know about
the invitation? Are you putting off the invitation?

_____

_____

_____

_____

_____

_____

_____

_____

_____

_____

No Longer Prisoners

Many of us have accepted Jesus as our Lord and Savior but
are still being held as prisoners to the lie that anxiety has to
stay or that fear is a part of who we are and we are simply

going to need to figure out how we can manage until Jesus comes back. This lie robs us of the life that Jesus specifically came for us to live. Not only are we given salvation through Jesus Christ, but we are invited to taste and see the heart of God in every aspect of our lives.

Just as I either forgot or put aside opening up my envelope, many of us forget the blessings that God has for us while we live here on earth. Other times, we do not realize the power of the invitation, and so opening it loses its place of priority in our lives. God has invited you to His peace that "surpasses all understanding" (Philippians 4:7, ESV)—and so anxiety does not have to lead your life. God has invited you to His joy that is strong (Nehemiah 8:10) and His hope that is secure (Hebrews 6:19)—and so depression does not have to be your label. God has invited you to freedom and faith—fear does not have to dictate every decision you make. When we are told that we have been invited to accept every spiritual blessing in Christ, this means that starting today, the authority to dance in the life of God belongs to us.

We truly discover who we were meant to be when we walk in the One who purposefully made us, and He is inviting each of us to walk with Him. The temporary invitations of this world cannot compare to the invitation that God has personally extended to us.

What do you think about God having abundant life in store for you today (John 10:10, ESV)? This life doesn't start when we arrive in heaven, but it starts as soon as we accept His invitation. In what areas of your life might this apply?

_____

_____

_____

_____

_____

_____

_____

_____

DEAR GOD, THANK YOU FOR INVITING ME TO HAVE A GENUINE RELATIONSHIP WITH YOU. HELP ME WALK IN THE FREEDOM THAT I HAVE IN YOU TODAY INSTEAD OF BEING TRAPPED IN THE LIE THAT I HAVE TO WAIT UNTIL HEAVEN TO EXPERIENCE TRUE FREEDOM IN YOU.

You have the
POWER to
speak LIGHT
& LIFE into
the hearts
of those
AROUND you.

THE WEIGHT OF
THE WORDS

Gracious words are a honeycomb,
sweet to the soul and healing to the bones.

PROVERBS 16:24

The Power of Life and Death

When God said, "Let there be light," there was light (Genesis 1:3). When He said, "Let the land produce living creatures," it happened (Genesis 1:24). Just as God spoke life into existence, we have the same power to speak life into other people because we've invited Him into our hearts. It has been so sweet to see what God does through the simplest encounters I have. I have passed by precious folks and told them that their hair looked nice, that they looked beautiful that day, and that they were awesome, and countless times I have had people come up to me to let me know that that simple encounter completely turned their day around.

Our words hold so much value and weight. It can take

many compliments to balance out one negative remark. It is crazy how if we post something on social media and bucketloads of comments are filled with positivity and love, it's still the one negative comment that we remember. So remember that it also works the other way around—we have the power to speak death into others too. The power of life and death is in our tongues (Proverbs 18:21).

Scripture teaches us to treat others the way that we would want to be treated and that kind words are like honey, sweet to the soul and healing to the bones (Matthew 7:12; Proverbs 16:24). Words that are wholesome benefit those who are listening (Ephesians 4:29). You have the power to speak light and life and benefits and healing and sweetness into the hearts of those around you. The amazing gifts that dwell within you were not meant to be kept to yourself. Jesus spoke, and there was healing. Jesus spoke, and the dead rose to life. He spoke, and hearts of stone were changed to hearts of flesh. Jesus spoke, and joy replaced sorrow. Jesus spoke, and encouragement demolished discouragement. He spoke, and miracles defeated the situations that seemed impossible to overcome. He spoke, and wisdom rebuked foolishness, truth claimed victory over deceit, dry souls were refreshed, insecurity was conquered with genuine confidence, and love spoke unfailing power over hatred.

How have you been using the power of life and death lately? Are you following Jesus' example?

_____

_____

_____

_____

_____

_____

_____

_____

Speak Life over Others

Before Jesus went back to heaven, He told the disciples that we would do the works He did and that even greater things shall be done (John 14:12)! Such beauty did not happen only in the Bible—the Bible is alive and active today, living in you. Because of Jesus, you can speak healing and joy and encouragement and love and life and confidence and refreshment and truth and wisdom and miracles over those around you. This can be as simple as telling someone how lovely their smile is, how beautiful they are, how proud you are of them, how much God loves them. Speaking life into someone can be the sweet genuineness of asking them how their day is going and truly caring.

After I meet people, I often pray, *God, please help me to remember their fantastic name*, because I know that God calls me by name and this is so significant. So that is something I want to do for others—I want to call them by their anointed and special name. Everyone has priceless beauty fearfully and wonderfully knitted within them (Psalm 139:13-14), but so many have no idea that this beauty exists. As God's chosen people, we are called to be the ones who let others know how beautiful they are because God made them that way.

What kind of words do you speak over others? How have you been reflecting God's light and love into their lives?

_____

_____

_____

_____

_____

_____

_____

_____

_____

_____

_____

Speak Life over Yourself

We have the power of life and death in the words that we are speaking over others—but also over ourselves. We listen and dwell on the words that we speak over ourselves, and these words hold great significance. I know that sometimes the words that I speak over myself are not words of light, and they can be very hurtful and mean. To speak plainly, when I do this, I am speaking death over myself. Whether or not I realize it, this is very powerful. But there is greater power in speaking words that are wholesome and that benefit our listening ears.

There is power in believing that we are who God says we are, and we find freedom and life when our conversations with ourselves align with the words that God speaks over us. May the words we speak over ourselves and the words that we speak over others benefit those who listen.

What words of life has God spoken over you? What words do you speak over you?

_____

_____

_____

_____

_____

_____

_____

_____

DEAR GOD, THANK YOU FOR BLESSING ME
WITH THE ABILITY TO SPEAK. "MAY THESE WORDS OF MY
MOUTH AND THIS MEDITATION OF MY HEART BE PLEASING [AND
ACCEPTABLE] IN YOUR SIGHT" BECAUSE YOU ARE MY "LORD, MY
ROCK AND MY REDEEMER" (PSALM 19:14). HELP ME TO
BE WISE IN THE WORDS I SPEAK, SPEAKING ONLY TO
BUILD OTHERS UP AND TO BRING YOU PRAISE.

FAITHFUL IN
THE FURNACE

*We fix our eyes not on what is seen, but on what is
unseen, since what is seen is temporary,
but what is unseen is eternal.*

2 CORINTHIANS 4:18

Fiery Trials

When a silversmith is going through the awesome process of refining and purifying silver, he breaks the rock
and places it into a crucible, a container that metal can be
placed in under the circumstance of very high tempera-
tures. The silversmith puts the crucible in a furnace and
holds the silver in the fire until all impurities are removed.
When the silversmith's reflection can be seen in the silver,
then the refining and purifying is complete.

God is our silversmith holding us in the fire, and the
fact that He allows us to go through trials is one of the
many reasons that He is so good. We all have times when
we are in the crucible, times that can be so hard and can
make it so easy for us to question or even blame God for

what we can see with our own eyes. But He is close to the brokenhearted, and He allows us to walk through heat and pressure because He knows that if we fix our eyes on Him, we will be mature and complete, not lacking anything, a reflection of Him (Psalm 34:18; James 1:4). He promises to finish the good work that He started in us, and He promises to work all things together for the good of those who love Him and are called according to His purpose (Philippians 1:6; Romans 8:28).

What are some fiery circumstances you've been facing? What is your response to being in the fire?

_____

_____

_____

_____

_____

_____

_____

_____

_____

_____

_____

_____

With Us in the Fire

In Daniel 3, three young Hebrew men named Shadrach, Meshach, and Abednego chose to not bow down to a big statue because they only bowed down to the Lord. Because of their decision to do this, the king of Babylon ordered the guards to throw these three into a fiery furnace. The young men responded to the king by saying, "If we are thrown into the blazing furnace, the God we serve is able to deliver us from it, and he will deliver us from Your Majesty's hand. But even if he does not, we want you to know, Your Majesty, that we will not serve your gods or worship the image of gold you have set up" (verses 17-18).

What a powerful response to the furnaces of our lives! We are called to declare in the face of a trial that our God is still who He says He is, and He will deliver us from the fire, but we are so confident in Him that even if He does not save us, we are still not going to bow down to the things of

GOD allows us to WALK through heat & pressure to MAKE us mature & complete.

this world. This rich trust in the Lord is unshaken because God cannot be shaken.

When he heard Shadrach, Meshach, and Abednego's response, the king became so furious that "he ordered the furnace heated seven times hotter than usual and commanded some of the strongest soldiers . . . to tie [the men] up . . . and throw them into the blazing furnace" (verses 19-20). But after they were thrown into the furnace, the king jumped up, amazed. He saw them walking around freely, with no injuries—and with a fourth who looked like the son of the gods. Quickly, the king called the young men to come out, and as they did, there was no sign on them that they had just walked out of a furnace. Then the king began to praise God (verses 24-28).

Even as you are walking into the fiery furnace and flames are getting seven times hotter, do not bow down to the temptation of believing that God has left you. He is with you in the fiery furnace, and you will not be burned!

What do you see about God's heart when you hear that He is with you in the furnaces of your life?

_____

_____

_____

_____

_____

_____

_____

_____

A Faithful Walk

Faith is being confident "in what we hope for" and certain "about what we do not see" (Hebrews 11:1). There will be people who see you being held in the fire, being refined to reflect who Jesus is, and they will come to praise Him because they will see His reflection in you. Jesus said that we do not understand what He is doing now, but one day we will understand (John 13:7). In Him you can set your eyes not on what is seen but, rather, on what is unseen because you know that what is seen is just temporary and what is unseen is eternal (2 Corinthians 4:18).

He has not left you. He has not forgotten you. He has not abandoned you. You are His dearest treasure, and the compassion that He has on you goes above and beyond your knowledge. God is bringing his goodness and beauty to completion in and through you for His glory, so don't quit. Nothing is done just to be done. God has a purpose and a plan to prosper us and not to harm us, plans to give us "a hope and a future" (Jeremiah 29:11). Even when we walk through the furnace, we shall "fear no evil," because He is here (Psalm 23:4)—and the hardships of the furnace cannot even compare to the joy that is coming (Romans 8:18). In this promise, we have the assurance that nothing will overcome us when we are walking with God. May we consider it "pure joy . . . whenever [we] face trials of many kinds, because [we] know that the testing of [our] faith produces perseverance." So we must "let perseverance finish its work so that [we] may be mature and complete, not lacking anything" (James 1:2-4).

When people see you in the midst of suffering, do they begin to praise God because they see in your response that He is with you? What are some ways you can begin to walk more faithfully in trials?

_____

_____

_____

_____

_____

_____

_____

_____

DEAR GOD, YOU ARE FAITHFUL, AND I TRUST YOU
EVEN WHEN I CANNOT SEE WHAT IS ON THE OTHER SIDE
OF THIS TRIAL. PLEASE HELP ME TO CONSIDER IT PURE JOY
WHEN I FACE TRIALS OF MANY KINDS, BECAUSE I KNOW THAT
THE TESTING OF MY FAITH PRODUCES PERSEVERANCE. HELP
ME TO LET PERSEVERANCE FINISH ITS WORK SO THAT
I MAY BE MATURE AND COMPLETE, NOT LACKING
ANYTHING. YOU ARE SO GOOD.

NOT FOR A RESPONSE

Whatever you do, work at it with all your heart,
as working for the Lord, not for human masters.

COLOSSIANS 3:23

Monitors

One day I went to work out with my beautiful momma, and this was at a time in my life when I was fearful of running on the treadmill. I was not at the running stage yet. Catch how lovely and encouraging the word *yet* is. We should not be hard on ourselves when we are not where we hope to one day be but, rather, embrace the journey that God has us on to get there. He wants to teach us things in the process. So, purposefully, I was walking on the treadmill beside my momma. This was when I first began to really try out this workout machine, and I started to enjoy it pretty quickly because God began to show me something through this treadmill.

At the workout place we went to, we were each given a monitor. This monitor connects to a screen at the front of the gym that basically shows how hard each person is working based on the calories they are burning, their heart rate, and so on. I apparently did not have my monitor on correctly, and because of this, the screen at the front of the room was showing that I wasn't doing anything. This made me smile so big because whatever we do, we do it in Jesus' name with all of our hearts as we are working for the Lord and not for man. I was working hard, but the screen did not say so, and the screen was what everybody could see.

Often, we allow our identity, our validation, and our progress to be determined by what is seen on a screen by others. This could be found through the number of likes that we get on social media or in any way that is filtered through the approval of people. But the moment that we begin to take action and start running on our own strength so that we can get the applause of people and the spotlight from a screen is the moment that we have missed the whole purpose.

Do you ever "monitor" your work for the Lord and look to see if others are noticing? Do you ever find yourself serving others, expecting a response of gratitude?

_____

_____

_____

_____

_____

_____

_____

_____

_____

_____

_____

Serving like Jesus

In Luke 17:11-19, Jesus was traveling to Jerusalem one day, and He was going into a village. From a distance, ten men with leprosy stood and called out in a loud voice saying, "Jesus, Master, have pity on us!" He cleansed all ten of them, but only one came to thank Him. Jesus knew that only one out of the ten would thank Him, and He still chose to heal them—because He wanted His Father to get all of the praise.

In the same way, Jesus came and died for all of the sins of the world. He came and died and rose again so that every single person might have a way to eternally be with the Father. He knew that there would be some who would not

True JOY
is when
we SERVE
the LORD
by serving
OTHERS.

believe in Him, and even so, He died, fully loving each and every one of us.

Sometimes you will act kindly and show love and step out of your comfort zone to bring encouragment to others without acknowledgment. Sometimes you will not receive a thank-you. But we are not called to love people and live in obedience to God so that people will tell us thank you or so that we will be noticed on a screen. God is looking at our hearts, and He is looking for hearts that want Him to be noticed and for Him to be praised.

What does it mean to you when you read that Jesus came to die for us, knowing that some of us would reject Him?

_____

_____

_____

_____

_____

_____

_____

_____

_____

_____

In Secret

True joy in living for the Lord is when we serve Him by serving others and could care less if anyone ever knew our name. Our focus must be that His name be made known among the hearts of all people because it is all about Him. May we be a people who love and serve and give and work wholeheartedly because of who God is and because it is His approval that we are seeking and He is who we are living for.

"But when you give to the needy, do not let your left hand know what your right hand is doing, so that your giving may be done in secret. Then your Father, who sees what is done in secret, will reward you" (Matthew 6:3-4). We should not serve others so we can boast in what we do but, rather, so we can boast in how good the Lord is (2 Corinthians 10:17). He is why we cannot help but serve. For example, I don't pay for the person behind me in the drive-through so that they will know my name but so that they can get a glimpse of who God is by my loving them in that way. This life is not for a screen, but it is for Him to be seen through us.

Who can you serve today without expecting a response from them, simply doing it because you love them? How can you love and serve in quiet ways?

_____

_____

_____

_____

_____

_____

_____

_____

DEAR GOD, THANK YOU FOR LOVING ME
EVEN WHEN MY RESPONSE TO YOU IS NOT ALWAYS THE
BEST. HELP ME TO LOVE OTHERS WITHOUT AN AGENDA BUT
SIMPLY BECAUSE YOU LOVED ME FIRST.

Prayer is POWERFUL because it is SEEKING the face of the ONE for whom nothing is IMPOSSIBLE.

THE POWER OF PRAYER

When you ask, you must believe and not doubt,
because the one who doubts is like a wave of the sea,
blown and tossed by the wind. That person should not
expect to receive anything from the Lord.

JAMES 1:6-7

Ask Boldly

A couple of years ago the Lord put it on my heart to ask Him for speaking opportunities. Specifically, He laid it on my heart to ask Him for twelve speaking opportunities that year—one a month. In James 1:6-7, we are told that when we ask, we "must believe and not doubt, because the one who doubts is like a wave of the sea, blown and tossed by the wind. That person should not expect to receive any-thing from the Lord." And in John 14:14, Jesus tells us to ask anything in His name and He will do it. This is very beautiful because when we walk with Jesus and take delight in Him, the desires of our hearts begin to align with His, so therefore, we begin to want what God wants. To boldly ask anything in the name of Jesus is to ask in faith according to His will.

So, in excited confidence, I asked the Lord in January to bless me with the opportunity to open His Word and speak twelve times that year. Someone called and asked if I could come and speak at a conference in January. We got an e-mail asking if I could speak at a retreat in February, and we got a message asking if I could come speak at an event in March. I then went to speak in April and began to praise God for September because I knew that He had gone before me and been faithful. I spoke every month that year, and sometimes twice a month, because God loves to blow us away and make His name known.

What has God laid on your heart to ask for boldly?

_____

_____

_____

_____

_____

_____

Devoted

In Colossians 4:2, Paul tells the believers, "Devote yourselves to prayer, being watchful and thankful," and the way that this verse builds is so encouraging. To devote yourself to something means to attend constantly. "The prayer of a righteous person is powerful and effective," and because God bends down to listen, we shall pray as long as we have breath (James 5:16; Psalm 116:2). Jesus is the way to the Father, and because Jesus died on the cross and rose from the grave to conquer our sins that separate us from God, the veil is torn and we now have complete access to the presence of God (Hebrews 10:19-20). We can "approach God's throne of grace with confidence" (Hebrews 4:16). To devote ourselves to prayer means to talk with Him all of the time.

Sometimes it is easy to get into the habit of praying simple prayers such as thanking God for this day or for the meal we are about to eat or asking Him to help us do well on a test. While these prayers are beautiful, God has so much more that He wants to give to us and through us in our prayers. In devoting ourselves to prayer, we are committed to talking with the Father, and our faith deepens as we see how He is able to do exceedingly and abundantly more than what we could ever ask or imagine according to His power at work within us (Ephesians 3:20).

What does it look like for you to be devoted in prayer? What times could you use for prayer that you currently use for something else?

_____

_____

_____

_____

_____

_____

_____

_____

_____

Not only do we get to devote our lives to talking with God, but we are also called to be watchful. If we are being watchful for something, then we have a sense of expectancy and alertness. We would not be looking for something that we were not expecting to come, so to be watchful in our prayers, we are not looking to see if God will answer but simply how He will.

The Lord has gone before us and has been faithful in ways that we have not even seen yet, and He hears us while we are still speaking, and He answers us before we even call on Him (Isaiah 65:24). Therefore, we praise Him before we have even seen our prayers answered, and we thank Him "in all circumstances" (1 Thessalonians 5:18)! We enter His presence with thanksgiving (Psalm 100:4), and because we are always in His presence, we should always be thankful.

In Joshua 10, Joshua is leading the Israelite army to fight against the five kings of the Amorites. The Lord had told the Israelites to not be afraid of them because He had given them into their hands and that not one of them would be able to withstand the Israelites (Joshua 10:8). The sun was going down, and Joshua needed more daylight to take hold of the victory that the Lord had already gone before and given into his hands. So "Joshua said to the Lord in the presence of Israel: 'Sun, stand still over Gibeon, and you, moon, over the Valley of Aijalon.' So the sun stood still, and the moon stopped, till the nation avenged itself on its enemies" (Joshua 10:12-13). The sun literally stopped in the middle of the sky and delayed going down about a full day (Joshua 10:13)! How incredible!

Joshua was devoted to prayer and prayed with expectant faith and was watchful, and while I do not know what Joshua's response was because the Word does not tell us, I would think that he was so thankful. Prayer is powerful because it is seeking the face of the One who is holy and for whom nothing is impossible.

Are there prayers you have prayed that you are being watchful in faith for God to answer? What are they? What can you thank God for in advance, even before seeing how He answers your prayer?

_____

_____

_____

_____

_____

_____

_____

_____

_____

_____

_____

_____

_____

⌒

DEAR GOD, THANK YOU FOR BLESSING ME
WITH THE ABILITY TO TALK WITH YOU ALWAYS BECAUSE OF
JESUS. TEACH ME HOW TO BE BOLD, DEVOTED, WATCHFUL, AND
THANKFUL AS I PRAY. SHOW ME WHAT YOU WANT ME TO
PRAY ABOUT WHEN I AM THINKING TOO SMALL, AND
HELP ME TO TRUST THAT THERE IS NOTHING
THAT IS IMPOSSIBLE FOR YOU.

JESUS is
our Prince of
PEACE, & we
must let
HIM rule.

CONSIDER THE BIRDS

*Look at the birds of the air; they do not sow or reap
or store away in barns, and yet your heavenly Father
feeds them. Are you not much more valuable than they?*

MATTHEW 6:26

Wooed by His Love

God is always wooing us with His unfailing love. He lavishes us with His reckless love that we do not deserve, though we are made to receive it. He is our Pursuer and He loves to romance us with all that He is and all that we are in Him. A mentor of mine once brought to my attention the truth that God woos us because He is our Beloved and we are His.

One of the many ways that He woos me with His love is through the birds. I smile when I see them. In Matthew 6 Jesus tells us not to worry about our lives, not to worry about what we will eat or drink or about our bodies and what we will wear. Indeed, our lives are more than food, and our bodies are more than clothes. With compassion, He simply encourages us and says to look at the birds that fly in the air; they don't plant food or save it for later, but still our heavenly Father feeds them. "Are you not much more valuable than they?" He asks. By worrying we do not add a single hour to our lives (verses 25-27). I have been walking before and have seen birds flying above, and I have begun to cry in joy and gratitude, knowing that God was reminding me that He is the One who takes care of me. Because He is not worried, I do not need to worry.

How does God woo you with His love?

_____

_____

_____

_____

_____

_____

_____

_____

_____

_____

_____

_____

Seek Him First

Jesus' statement that we should not worry is not simply a suggestion or an opinion—it is a command that He is giving us. Jesus commands us not to worry because to worry means to take our eyes off of the One who is our Provider, and it is to stop seeking Him first. This is why He continues, "But seek first his kingdom and his righteousness, and all these things will be given to you as well" (Matthew 6:33). He knows that when we seek Him first, we will experience His peace that surpasses all understanding (Philippians 4:7). You cannot have both peace and worry at the same time.

Jesus said in John 14:27 that He has given us His peace and He has left it with us. He does not "give to [us] as the world gives," therefore we shall not "let [our] hearts be troubled." The peace Jesus is talking about can only come from seeking Him first. God tells us not to worry about anything. If He takes care of the birds, won't He also take care of us, who are so much more valuable to Him? In order to walk in this peace, we must seek the Giver of peace first in all circumstances.

What are some areas where you are tempted to worry? How can you seek the Giver of peace more fully in them?

_____

_____

_____

_____

_____

_____

_____

_____

_____

_____

Let Peace Rule

In Colossians 3:15, we are told to "let the peace of Christ rule in [our] hearts" because we are "members of one body" and "called to peace." What a beautiful thing to be called to! What a wonderful thing to be ruled by. When someone rules, that person has authority and declares what actions are taken and what actions are not taken. When we worry, we are choosing to reject the rule of peace, but Jesus is our Prince of Peace (Isaiah 9:6), and we must let Him rule.

Next time you see a bird, I pray that you will laugh because the heavenly Father is wooing you in His love and leading you to remember that it is silly to worry. He is your Provider, and in Him alone you "lack no good thing" (Psalm 34:10). He cares for you, and He did not send His one and only Son to die for you so that you would live a life of worry. He came so that you may have life and have it abundantly (John 10:10). You can cast all of your cares and anxieties on Him "because He cares for you" (1 Peter 5:7). "He will sustain you" and promises that He will never permit the righteous to be shaken (Psalm 55:22). So beloved one, consider the birds today (Matthew 6:26).

Are you letting God's peace rule in your heart? In what areas of your life do you need to consider the birds right now?

_____

_____

_____

_____

_____

_____

_____

_____

_____

DEAR GOD, THANK YOU FOR ROMANCING ME. LORD, INDEED YOUR LOVE IS SO SWEET AND PASSIONATE. WHEN I AM LEANING TOWARD WORRY, PLEASE HELP ME TO REMEMBER THAT YOU ARE MY FATHER WHO CARES FOR ME. YOU ARE MY PROVIDER, AND I LACK NO GOOD THING IN YOU. THANK YOU FOR MEETING MY EVERY NEED ABOVE AND BEYOND.

I *WILL* SING

I will sing to the Lord all my life;
I will sing praise to my God as long as I live.

PSALM 104:33

Choose to Sing

My dad and I sing about everything. One time we started singing our own song about how we were excited about all things. We sing in the kitchen. We sing in the car. We sing everywhere we go. When I am away from home, we will sometimes sing to each other on the phone and hold out the notes just to really emphasize our joy, and then we start laughing so hard. Psalm 16:11 says that in God's presence is fullness of joy, and this joy is experienced in such a sweet and powerful way when we choose to join Him in the song He personally invites us to sing with Him.

I love how often God's Word speaks about singing to Him and making a new song to Him. Over and over again, I have read these verses: "I will sing and make music" (Psalm 57:7), "At his sacred tent I will sacrifice with shouts of joy;

I will sing and make music to the LORD" (Psalm 27:6), "I will sing the praises of the name of the LORD Most High" (Psalm 7:17), and "I will sing to the LORD all my life; I will sing praise to my God as long as I live" (Psalm 104:33). In these verses, the psalmist specifically declares that he *will* sing to the Lord. This is a choice that he makes regardless of what he is going through because he knows that the Lord is always worthy of praise.

Whether or not you will pray and sing hymns to God is a choice that you get to make. No one else can make this decision for you, and God is not focused on the pitch of your voice but rather the posture of your heart. He says that the "joy of the LORD is [our] strength" (Nehemiah 8:10), and to be joyful is not to be naive or inexperienced but to be aware that you are in the presence of the Lord. When we sing to Him, we step into an awareness of being in His presence, and we remember that He is worthy—and that will fill our hearts with joy.

What is the song in your heart? What does it mean for God to be worthy of all of the praise?

_____

_____

_____

_____

_____

_____

_____

_____

_____

Power in Praise

There is joy in praising God, and there is also power in our praise. In Acts 16, Paul and Silas were severely flogged, put in prison after rebuking a spirit in Jesus' name, and guarded carefully. At midnight, they "were praying and singing hymns to God, and the other prisoners were listening to them. Suddenly there was such a violent earthquake that the foundations of the prison were shaken. At once all of the prison doors flew open, and everyone's chains came loose" (verses 16-26).

It did not matter where Paul and Silas were; they chose to sing praises to God because they knew that God was worthy. The other prisoners were listening closely because it did not make sense for Paul and Silas to respond in the way that they did. In the same way, others will incline to

GOD is not focused on the PITCH of your VOICE but rather the POSTURE of your HEART.

listen to your praise, wondering why you are singing. There is power in your praise to God; indeed, your praise to the Lord breaks chains. Not only will the Lord deliver you through your praise, but He will use your praise to break the chains of those around you who are listening.

How might God use your praise to change your heart and break your chains? How might the song you sing to the Lord impact those who are around you?

_____

_____

_____

_____

_____

_____

_____

_____

_____

Our praise redirects the focus back to the Lord who is worthy and who is the One who gives us the strength to sing—not only in the good times but also in the times when we feel like we are chained in a prison cell at midnight. But this kind of response can only happen when we are aware that the Lord is rejoicing over us with loud singing.

Zephaniah 3:17 tells us that "the LORD your God is with you, the Mighty Warrior who saves. He will take great delight in you; in his love he will no longer rebuke you but will rejoice over you with singing." To fully believe He delights in us is to join Him in song regardless of what troubles lie ahead.

There is power in our praise because it is joining in the acknowledgment with all of creation that He is exalted over all and that He has the power to break every chain—the chains of anxiety, the chains of fear, the chains of shame. Yes, indeed, there is no prison foundation that He cannot shake. This is the confidence we have in the One who saved us and who sings over us.

How does knowing that God sings over us change your view of trials?

_____

_____

_____

_____

_____

_____

_____

_____

_____

_____

_____

DEAR GOD, THANK YOU FOR BEING MY
MIGHTY WARRIOR WHO HAS SAVED ME AND REJOICES
OVER ME WITH LOUD SINGING AND QUIETS MY HEART WITH
YOUR LOVE. YOU ARE SO GOOD TO ME, SO HELP ME TO ALWAYS
SING OF YOUR GOODNESS. HELP ME TO BOLDLY AND JOYFULLY
HAVE YOUR PRAISE ON MY LIPS NO MATTER WHERE I AM.
SHOW ME THE SONG THAT YOU HAVE PERSONALLY
WRITTEN ON MY HEART.

A heart
after GOD'S
own heart
is being
RENEWED
daily.

UNFADING BEAUTY

Your beauty should not come from outward adornment,
such as elaborate hairstyles and the wearing of gold
jewelry or fine clothes. Rather, it should be that of your
inner self, the unfading beauty of a gentle and quiet
spirit, which is of great worth in God's sight.

1 PETER 3:3-4

Trendy or Timeless?

Have you ever felt pressured to wear a certain outfit because it aligned with the current trends? Maybe it seemed as though everyone else was wearing that outfit, but something about it did not settle right with your heart when you looked in the mirror. Maybe you felt pressured because you thought that wearing something more revealing would grab a boy's attention or would cause you to be invited to hang out with a certain group of people, and all you wanted was to belong and to be noticed.

In 1 Peter 3:3-4, Peter speaks about fashion, with the power of the Holy Spirit, telling us that our beauty should not come from fancy hair or expensive gold jewelry or nice clothes. "Rather, it should be that of your inner self, the unfading beauty of a gentle and quiet spirit, which is of great worth in God's sight." How we clothe our hearts will overflow into the decisions we make regarding how we clothe our bodies. Solomon warns us, "Above all else, guard your heart, for everything that you do flows from it" (Proverbs 4:23), including the clothes that we wear.

God sees the beauty of your heart as unfading and precious. What does this say about Him? How does it affect how you think about what to wear?

_____

_____

_____

_____

_____

_____

_____

_____

_____

_____

_____

_____

Adorned

I love how God always addresses what is in a person's heart instead of simply talking about the symptoms of an issue because He knows that everything that we do flows from what is in our hearts. God is so personal, and He cares so much about us. This is why in Colossians 3:12-14, Paul says, "Clothe yourselves with compassion, kindness, humility, gentleness, and patience. . . . And over all these virtues put on love, which binds them all together in perfect unity."

When we adorn our heart with the heart of God, we will begin to reflect Him in all that we do—including our wardrobe. To adorn our hearts with God's heart is to walk hand in hand with Him and live wholeheartedly for Him. Our beauty does not come from outward adornment. Makeup and pretty dresses and jewelry are so much fun, but they are not our true source of beauty, and the affirmation of others is not our source of belonging. I just adore how what is precious in God's sight is a gentle and quiet spirit and that it holds unfading beauty. "Charm is deceptive, and beauty is fleeting; but a woman who fears the LORD is to be praised," and this is because a godly heart is so attractive (Proverbs 31:30). Outward beauty only lasts for a little while, but a heart after God's own heart is being renewed daily, and it blesses other people. This is a trend that will never go out of style.

If your heart had a style of clothing, what would it look like? What are some ways you can adorn your heart with God's heart?

_____

_____

_____

_____

_____

_____

_____

_____

_____

_____

_____

A Gentle Spirit

Peter also tells us to have a gentle and quiet spirit, but what does this mean? It is not to be reserved or to keep to yourself or to be someone who never speaks up, but rather it is to be confident in who the Lord has made you to be and to know that He has called you by name. He has engraved you upon the palm of His hand (Isaiah 49:16), and this is your belonging, and this is your beauty. In this world, you will have different labels and expectations targeting your heart, but when you know who you are in Christ, you do not have to become loud and chaotic with the world. Rather, your heart can remain peaceful and still because you already know who you are and whose you are.

In this chapter, I purposefully made no lists of what to wear and what not to wear because whatever we dress our hearts with will overflow into what we dress our bodies with. There is a sweet and powerful transformation that takes place when we know who we are in Christ, because we begin to dress to honor the Lord instead of dressing to impress the world.

Are you dressing to impress the world or dressing to express the Word? What does it mean to you to have a gentle and quiet spirit?

_____

_____

_____

_____

_____

_____

_____

_____

DEAR GOD, THANK YOU FOR SEEING MY HEART
AND FOR LOVING ME UNCONDITIONALLY. HELP ME TO CLOTHE
MY HEART WITH YOUR HEART BECAUSE I KNOW THAT THIS WILL
OVERFLOW INTO HOW I DRESS ON THE OUTSIDE. GIVE ME A
GENTLE AND QUIET SPIRIT THAT NEVER FADES AND IS
PRECIOUS IN YOUR SIGHT.

TIME TO JUMP

If the Son sets you free,
you will be free indeed.

JOHN 8:36

No Longer Prisoners

When an elephant is first trained, the trainer puts a chain around its ankle, and this way it cannot be free. The elephant remains where it is, and after a while, the trainer will put the smallest rope around the elephant's ankle. This rope is so weak that the elephant could snap it easily, but the elephant still believes that the chain is there, and therefore it won't break free even though it has complete power to do so.

In the same way, we have been given complete power to walk in the beauty that God has personally called us to, but instead many of us believe that we are still prisoners to our past, prisoners to our thought patterns, prisoners to our old lives. But this is a lie. The psalmist David prayed this way, "Set me free from my prison, that I may praise your name" (Psalm 142:7).

So often we live based on what is not true. If the Son sets us free, then we are free indeed (John 8:36), but some of us are still living as slaves to fear, when His perfect love has cast out all fear (1 John 4:18). Jesus has offered us something worth far more than silver or gold. In Him we can operate in the true purpose that God fearfully and wonderfully made us for. Paul tells us, "It is for freedom that Christ has set us free. . . . Do not let yourselves be burdened again by a yoke of slavery" (Galatians 5:1).

Like the elephants, what chains are you convinced are still around your ankle? How does knowing that Christ set us free change your perspective?

_____

_____

_____

_____

_____

No Longer Lame

One afternoon Peter and John were going up to the temple. There was a lame man being carried to the gate called Beautiful to beg from anyone who would be passing him by as they went in and out of the temple courts. He saw Peter and John as they were coming in his direction, and just as he did with many others who passed by, he begged from them and asked for money. Peter and John looked straight at him. (Isn't it incredible how they gave him their full attention, just as God gives us His full attention?) Peter told the man to look at him, and the man did, thinking that they were about to give him something (Acts 3:1-5).

Little did the man know that they were not about to give him something that would take care of him temporarily, but they were about to bless him exceedingly

Through JESUS we have been GIVEN the FREEDOM to walk & jump & praise GOD.

and abundantly more than what he could have ever asked or imagined according to the Lord's power at work. Acts 3:6-8 tells us, "Then Peter said, 'Silver or gold I do not have, but what I do have I give you. In the name of Jesus Christ of Nazareth, walk.' Taking him by the right hand, he helped him up, and instantly the man's feet and ankles became strong. He jumped to his feet and began to walk." The man then headed to the temple courts and began jumping and praising the Lord! Other people saw him and began to realize that this man was the same man who used to be lame. The same man who used to beg was now the man who was giving praise. The same man who used to not be able to walk was now jumping and praising God in an instant. There is nothing that God cannot do. They were awestruck at what they were witnessing (verses 8-10).

Through Jesus we have all been given the freedom to walk and jump and praise God, but we still live as though we are lame, paralyzed, and unable to be who God has called us to be. Just as Peter reached down and helped the lame man to his feet, Jesus came down and lifted us up so that we, too, can stand tall in hope that is not shaken.

In 2 Timothy 1:7, we are reminded that the spirit God has given us is not a spirit of fear or timidity but of "power, love and self-discipline." Because we are a new creation in Him and we no longer have to be prisoners to our old selves, we can stand up and walk and jump and praise God and actually experience all of the beauty that we were each uniquely designed to embrace and radiate (2 Corinthians 5:17).

God made us to jump and leap through His beauty and praise His name in freedom. What does this say about who He is?

_____

_____

_____

_____

_____

_____

_____

_____

_____

_____

_____

_____

Walk in Abundance

Through Christ, you have intentionally been given the power to walk in freedom. Because of Christ's undeniable and unfailing love for you, you have been given the freedom to love yourself and others just as He loves. You have the authority to jump into beauty with a mind that is self-disciplined in the truth to daily choose that His promises will be what are leading your steps. This is the spirit that you have been given. This is why when you operate out of fear, you will feel defeated or sometimes apathetic or even ineffective, and this is because the enemy's goal is to paralyze you with the belief that you can never experience God's beauty for your life. He wants to keep you in a place of apathy so that you will never taste and see the fun of praising God and leaping in all that He has done. He seeks to keep you from being effective.

After the man in Acts 3 began to walk and praise God, the people "were filled with wonder and amazement at what had happened to him" (verse 10). God not only calls you to freedom, but He also calls you to be a vessel of His freedom to lead others who are lame to begin walking and praising His name fully too. We have been given His Spirit to live abundantly in all that He has called us to and to lead others to stand up and be all that He has called them to be too. His love does not end with us, but His love continues with us. How beautiful it is to praise His name *fully*.

John and Peter boldly spoke the name of Jesus to cause the lame man to walk and jump. Who is spiritually lame around you that needs the power of Jesus?

_____

_____

_____

_____

_____

_____

_____

DEAR GOD, THANK YOU FOR BLESSING ME WITH FREEDOM THROUGH YOUR ONE AND ONLY SON, JESUS! YOU ARE WORTHY OF MY FULL PRAISE. LEAD ME TO JUMP AND DANCE IN THE FREEDOM THAT YOU HAVE GIVEN ME. YOU HAVE GIVEN ME COMPLETE AUTHORITY OVER THE ENEMY, SO PLEASE HELP ME TO WALK IN THIS AUTHORITY AND NOT REMAIN IN BONDAGE TO WHAT YOU HAVE SET ME FREE FROM.

EMBRACE THE WAIT

Those who hope in the Lord will renew their strength.
They will soar on wings like eagles; they will run and not
grow weary, they will walk and not be faint.

ISAIAH 40:31

Grow Roots

Chinese bamboo is quite peculiar and mighty neat, if you ask me. When a farmer plants bamboo, he provides sunlight and water consistently. A single cane grows for six to eight weeks and then stops growing. Then, for a whole year the farmer waters the plant with care, even though nothing more has shown on the plant. The second year a few new shoots will show up, while the farmer continues to water the plant. After another six to eight weeks, these shoots stop growing as well. A third year and a fourth year may pass without significant growth in the bamboo grove. But by the fifth year, new bamboo canes shoot up high in the sky and grow up to eighty feet tall in a matter of a few short weeks. During those four years where the farmer consistently cared for the bamboo, even though growth on the surface seemed slow, roots were growing strong beneath the soil in order to hold up the plant when difficult times came.

Sometimes our constant dedication to God can seem useless and unproductive because we cannot see the product we are looking forward to or working toward. But do not stop trusting in the Lord in this season of waiting—He is using it to help you put down roots. He tells us, "But those who wait for the Lord [who expect, look for, and hope in Him] will gain new strength and renew their power; they will lift up their wings [and rise up close to God] like eagles [rising toward the sun]; they will run and not become weary, they will walk and not grow tired" (Isaiah 40:31, AMP). He has not forgotten, and His Word does not return to Him until fulfilling the purpose for which He sent it (Isaiah 55:11). Not a single word from God will fail us (Luke 1:37).

What are you waiting for right now? How do you see the Lord after reading that He is not wasting this season of waiting?

_____

_____

_____

_____

_____

_____

_____

_____

_____

Trust God's Promises

Anyone can wait, but the posture of our hearts while we wait reveals whether or not we have patience. Patient people rejoice in the wait because they trust that the Lord's promises will faithfully come to full fruition in His perfect timing. The beauty of waiting is in knowing what God is orchestrating within us as we wait. We can be still and not fear, be strong, take heart, and wait for the Lord because He has made everything beautiful in its own time (Psalm 27:14; Ecclesiastes 3:11). God's timing is much different than ours, and this kind of different brings a lot of joy because He holds time in His hands. He just needs you to trust that He has you embraced in the security of His righteous wings and that He is deepening roots of His heart within you while you wait.

Do not miss this priceless opportunity for growth in the midst of waiting. Yes, the outcome of waiting and trusting

GOD has you EXACTLY where you NEED to BE.

is going to be outstanding and simply stunning, but what is cool is the flourishing gladness that God wants to grow from within you during this season right now. He wants to do something powerful while you wait.

Are you waiting in a rush, or are you waiting patiently? What is God doing in you while you wait?

_____

_____

_____

_____

_____

_____

_____

_____

_____

God hears you. He has gone before you and has been faithful and is leading you on the path that is best for His name's sake. In this season of waiting, He is building you up to become all that He made you originally to be. You may be in the first year or the fourth year, but be excited and expectant because God has you exactly where you need to be, and this is a reason to rejoice. God is sovereign in His timing, and He is not going to give you something that you are not yet ready to receive. He only wants you to have the best, and He knows that if you were to enter a season you are waiting for right now, you would be hurt because it simply isn't time. He is a good Father.

Seek God wholeheartedly and fear the Lord, for those who fear God and seek Him wholeheartedly lack no good thing (Psalm 34:9-10). Through the constant watering and sunlight and endurance that comes with waiting, God is right there with you and wants to show you the beauty in it. You will be amazed when you look back and see that because you were faithful in waiting, God has blown you away with blessings beyond your imagination that are better than anything you could have planned on paper. Jeremiah said, "The LORD is my portion; therefore I will wait for him" (Lamentations 3:24). What a sweet and satisfying place to be—so fully content in who God is and who you are in Him that there is hope in the times of waiting.

How can you rejoice in times of waiting? How do you think the way you wait impacts those around you?

_____

_____

_____

_____

_____

_____

_____

_____

DEAR GOD, YOU ARE TRUSTWORTHY, AND I
THANK YOU FOR WORKING ALL THINGS ACCORDING TO
MY GOOD AS I LOVE YOU AND AM CALLED ACCORDING TO YOUR
PURPOSE (ROMANS 8:28). TEACH ME TO BE PATIENT, TO TRUST
YOU, AND TO REJOICE IN TIMES OF WAITING, AND PLEASE
REVEAL TO ME GREAT AND UNSEARCHABLE THINGS THAT
I DO NOT KNOW AS I WAIT (DANIEL 2:22).

You are
GIVING others a
warm HUG by
simply BEING
HONEST with
them.

A WARM HUG

There is a time for everything,
and a season for every activity under the heavens . . .
a time to weep and a time to laugh, a time
to mourn and a time to dance.

ECCLESIASTES 3:1,4

Transparency

Sometimes people ask me, "Do you ever have a bad day?" or "Are you ever sad?" Hearing these questions, I find myself overthinking and focusing on two extremes. On the one hand, I can make transparency my goal by making it known when I had a bad day because I feel as though I have to show people that I do get sad. The problem is that in doing this, I zoom the focus in on my weaknesses and my sadness and gloom in such a way that they are made a much bigger deal than necessary. At the other extreme, I can become fearful of what others may think when they know I am going through something or feeling a certain way that doesn't look nice, so I try to hide it.

Neither one of these extremes is what God designed. Transparency is honesty—it is neither highlighting to people that I had a bad day nor hiding emotions that aren't pretty. Transparency is not letting my struggles be all I talk about because I want to make sure that I can "relate" to people. When I do that, I'm not being transparent—I'm worrying about other people's opinions.

To be transparent is to let go of dwelling on what others think or how they may see you and to simply be honest—honest with God, honest with yourself, and honest with others. There's no sugarcoating necessary. *The Message* puts it this way: "An honest answer is like a warm hug" (Proverbs 24:26). Some who receive your honesty will love it and others will despise it, but whether they realize it or not, you are giving them a warm hug by simply being honest with them.

How have you been honest with the Lord, with yourself, and with others about your struggles? When is it difficult to be honest?

_____

_____

_____

_____

_____

_____

_____

_____

_____

The Gift of Emotions

Jesus walked in transparency beautifully, and anytime I am looking for how to do something, I always look to see how Jesus did it. Jesus walked into the temple to see people buying and selling and disregarding the holiness of the house of His Father, and He began to rebuke them and flip tables (Matthew 21:12-13). When Jesus saw that His best friend, Lazarus, died, He wept (John 11:35). When Jesus went to meet the woman at the well in Samaria, John 4 says that He got there and was tired, so He had to sit down. He was compassionate toward people (Matthew 9:36). He was playful and kind as He said, "Let the little children come to me" (Matthew 19:14).

Solomon said it this way: there is "a time to weep and a time to laugh, a time to mourn and a time to dance" (Ecclesiastes 3:4). To have emotion is a gift. God gave us the gift of feelings and emotions. To hide them would be to hide a gift because we are each uniquely made in God's image, and therefore we each share our emotions in a unique way that reflects the heart of God. This does not mean that we need to make our decisions based on our emotions, but it does reveal that there is beauty and freedom about being honest with them. To speak the truth in love will bring people eternal joy if they are willing to receive it. To speak what everyone wants to hear will bring people temporary happiness that will only last a little while.

What emotions do you think of as "bad" emotions? How can you be honest about these emotions in a beautiful and free way?

_____

_____

_____

_____

_____

_____

_____

Permission to Be Honest

The enemy may feed you the lie that other people will not see you the same once you are honest with them or that your relationship with them will take a negative turn. Take a step back and see this statement through the lens of God's goodness: this statement is actually true when seen through the correct lens. People will not see you the same when you begin to be honest with them. They will view you with a deeper respect, and a door of influence will be opened like you could never have imagined. Your relationship with them will in fact look different because it will be deeper and sweeter, and people will begin to come to you knowing that they, too, can be real as they see you be real. People do not need your permission to be honest in who they are, but your being willing to step out of pride and fear in order to be transparent will help others feel as though they have permission to do so as well.

Let us be honest with one another—it is the same as giving a warm hug. Sometimes it will feel like others give us the cold shoulder in response, and sometimes we will be placed in a very awkward moment because of how we choose to be transparent. But let us joyfully step into those moments because not only does God want to show us freedom, but He also wants to use us to lead others to freedom. We are called to give warm hugs, and we do this by being transparent.

How might your honesty give others permission to share as well?

_____

_____

_____

_____

_____

_____

_____

_____

DEAR GOD, YOU ARE SO UNDERSTANDING. THERE
IS NOTHING ABOUT ME THAT YOU DO NOT KNOW AND THAT
YOU, JESUS, DO NOT EMPATHIZE WITH. THANK YOU FOR BLESSING
ME WITH FEELINGS AND EMOTIONS. HELP ME TO BE HONEST WITH
MYSELF AND HONEST WITH OTHERS ABOUT MY FEELINGS AND
EMOTIONS, BUT ALSO PLEASE HELP ME TO ALWAYS FILTER
MY EMOTIONS THROUGH YOUR WORD SO THAT IT IS
ONLY YOUR WORD THAT DETERMINES MY DECISIONS.

THE GOSPEL

If anyone is in Christ, the new creation has come:
The old has gone, the new is here!

2 CORINTHIANS 5:17

A Fall from Grace

In the very beginning God walked with Adam and Eve "in the cool of the day" through the Garden of Eden (Genesis 3:8). This has been His desire and design ever since, because God desires to walk with us daily, and He designed us to walk with Him daily. When God walked with Adam and Eve in the Garden of Eden, everything was perfect. There was complete union and peace between God and humankind. Nothing was separating them from one another.

God told Adam and Eve that they could eat of any tree in the Garden, except for one particular tree (Genesis 2:16-17). One day, the serpent came to Eve. The enemy deceived Eve, which led her to choose to disobey God and eat the fruit from the very tree that God told them not to eat from, and Adam also ate of the fruit. Adam and Eve sinned—they missed the mark. Because they disobeyed the Lord, they could no longer be with God and have a perfect relationship with Him because He is a holy and perfect God and their sin created a separation from Him (Genesis 3; Isaiah 59:2).

How has sin come between you and God, either in the past or currently?

_____

_____

_____

_____

_____

_____

_____

_____

_____

_____

_____

_____

A New Creation

Sin separated us, but God had a plan to redeem all of us back into a perfect relationship with Himself. The Bible says it this way: for God so loved you and me "that He gave His one and only Son, that whoever believes in Him shall not perish but have eternal life" (John 3:16). God demonstrated His perfect love for us "in that while we were still sinners, Christ died for us" (Romans 5:8, ESV). "The wages of sin is death, but the gift of God is eternal life in Christ Jesus our Lord" (Romans 6:23). Jesus came and lived the perfect life that none of us could or can live, and He died the death that we all deserve by taking on all of the sins of the world. Three days after He died, He rose from the grave, defeating death and the power of sin.

Because of the Cross, we are one in Christ just as Christ is one in the Father. This is why anyone who is in Christ is a new creation—"the old has passed away and behold,

GOD *had*
a PLAN *to*
redeem all of
US *back into*
a PERFECT
relationship
with HIMSELF.

the new has come" (2 Corinthians 5:17, ESV). God has not given us this gift of life and reunion through Jesus because of anything that we have done or by anything that we have not done but because of what Jesus already did. He is coming back one day to be enthroned as King forever, and there will be a new heaven and a new earth, and this is what we eagerly wait for. All who know Him will spend forever with Him and there will be no more sorrow and no more pain (2 Peter 3:13; Revelation 21:1-5).

How beautiful!

What do you see in the heart of God when you hear that He sent His only Son to die for you so that you could live with Him forever? What does it mean in your life for the old to be passed away and for the new to come?

_____

_____

_____

_____

_____

_____

Restored Relationship

Even in the midst of your sin, God still called you by name (Isaiah 43:1). Before time ever began, He saw you and loved you and chose you. While we were still sinners, Christ died for us because He desires to be in relationship with us and designed us to be in a relationship with Him.

Jesus loves you! He loves you so much that He meets you right now where you are, but He loves you way too much to leave you there. By confessing with your mouth and believing in your heart that Jesus is Lord, you will be saved (Romans 10:9). Oh my goodness, tears come to my eyes as I dwell on the undeserved love of God. Because of Jesus, you do not have to live the same way you have been. You do not have to keep running in the same circles and falling into sin, but in Him you can have abundant life!

The only response I can find to such news is to praise and worship Jesus all the days of my life! By giving my life to Jesus, I do not become perfect, and all of my problems don't disappear, but they are placed in the hands of the One who is perfect and who turns my problems into a testimony of His promises. Such a love makes me want to love. Such freedom makes me want to tell everyone I meet about Jesus who is the only Way, the only Truth, and the only Life.

Jesus died and rose again in triumph so that together we could forever be His. Behold, the old is gone and the new has come!

Do you have a personal relationship with Christ? Where do you see Him calling you closer to Himself?

_____

_____

_____

_____

_____

_____

_____

_____

_____

_____

_____

_____

_____

_____

_____

Dear God, thank You for demonstrating Your
perfect love for me in that while I was still a sinner,
Christ died for me. Though the wages of my sin is death,
You have given me the free gift of eternal life in Christ
Jesus! Thank You, God!!! I have tried to do life on my
own, and it simply doesn't work because You are the
Way, the Truth, and the Life. Teach me what it
looks like to walk as a new creation in You.

WHAT TIGGERS DO BEST

Go and make disciples of all nations,
baptizing them in the name of the Father and of
the Son and of the Holy Spirit, and teaching them to
obey everything I have commanded you. And surely
I am with you always, to the very end of the age.

MATTHEW 28:19-20

Excitedly Obedient

I love Winnie the Pooh! In Disney's Winnie the Pooh films, anytime Tigger is asked to do something, he responds with "That's what Tiggers do best!" For example, one time Roo asks him to climb trees, and he responds with, "That's what Tiggers do best!" He sings, "The wonderful thing about Tiggers is Tiggers are wonderful things!"

I think we can learn a lot from Tigger about being excitedly obedient in the ordinary. When you are willing to go and be obedient even in your everyday moments, that is when God will make it a miraculous supernatural moment for His glory. When God asked who would go speak His words, Isaiah said in the presence of the Lord, "Here I am,

215

send me" (Isaiah 6:8). In the same way, God is asking each of us to obey, and we begin to walk in our purpose and truly discover freedom when we obediently surrender to where God is wanting us to go.

The wonderful thing about you is that you are a wonderful thing. Your life is knitted with purpose, and you are a child of the one true King. You are truly, truly, truly, truly loved, loved, loved, loved, loved! But the most wonderful thing about you is that God uniquely made you to reach people for His name's sake in a way that no one else can.

What does it say about God that He made each of us unique but all for the same purpose—to glorify Him?

_____

_____

_____

_____

_____

_____

_____

In Mark 16:15, Jesus says, "Go into all the world and preach the gospel to all creation." This command can potentially be intimidating and overwhelming, and sometimes we won't even attempt it because we feel incapable of reaching the whole world. But you see, your world is wherever you currently are.

If you are in your home, your delighted honor is to see what chores need to be done and to do them, because that's what children of God do best. You can leave surprise notes of encouragement throughout your house, because that's what children of God do best. When you are at school and someone is sitting alone at lunch, you can sit with them, because that is what children of God do best. You can hold the door open and let others know how beautiful they are and how loved they are and how awesome they are, because that is what children of God do best. When you see trash on the ground, even though you didn't put it there, you can pick it up, because that is what children of God do best. When you are in the coffee shop, you can leave Scripture written on the receipt and pay for the person behind you, because that is what children of God do best. God is love, and by loving people extravagantly, you introduce God to them.

We make the name of JESUS famous by how WE love, live, serve, & speak.

How has God uniquely made you to love people? What are some additional ways you can love others extravagantly?

_____

_____

_____

_____

_____

_____

_____

_____

Tell Others

When you are being the hands and feet of Jesus to people, you will get many different responses. I remember one time I was sitting in the airport telling a beautiful lady about Jesus. She told me that I was wasting my breath and that she didn't believe. I have talked with people for hours on end about how awesome God is, and I have had people tell me straight faced that they do not think the love of God is for them. There are people all around us in the world wherever we currently are. Some know Him and love Him, some have heard about Him and don't think that He applies to them, and some want nothing to do with Him, but Jesus said, "Go and make disciples" (Matthew 28:19). This command is so comforting because God gave us His Spirit, the Holy Spirit, to be with us always and to lead us as we *go* and make His name known everywhere to everyone, one person at a time.

God blesses us so that we can bless others, and that is what children of God do best. We give hugs, we smile, we mourn with those who mourn, we listen and give with a cheerful heart. As children of God, we will go out into every square inch of the world and make the name of Jesus famous by how we love, how we live, how we serve, how we speak, and how we do what children of God do best.

Who do you know that you need to share Jesus with because they do not know Him? What words and actions has God given you to share with them?

_____

_____

_____

_____

_____

_____

_____

_____

_____

_____

_____

_____

_____

_____

DEAR GOD, THANK YOU FOR LOVING THE WHOLE
WORLD SO MUCH THAT YOU WOULD GIVE YOUR ONLY SON
FOR US. PLEASE HELP ME TO BE FAITHFUL TO BE YOUR VESSEL
WHEREVER I AM AND WHOEVER I AM WITH. I AM YOURS.
THANK YOU FOR BEING WITH ME ALWAYS.

ACKNOWLEDGMENTS

We have all been given different gifts by the Spirit, and each of us reveal the character and the strengths of God in such unique and sweet ways. When the Lord first placed the dream of writing this book on my heart, I did not foresee the many precious humans who would walk alongside me, seeking the Lord first with me in ways that powerfully revealed the faithfulness and provision and kindness of the Lord. These people were operating in the strengths personally given to them by God. They were practicing their gifts, and this was a blessing. Through the three years of writing and rewriting and editing and crying over and getting excited over and praying over these pages, these people sharpened me, encouraged me, believed in me, and prayed with me.

I would adore the honor of personally thanking these

world changers who walked with me and celebrated in God with me:

My mom, who inspires me and teaches me not only with the wisdom and kindness that comes off her tongue but through the way that she lives day by day. She champions me on in truth and unconditionally loves me because she knows that God first loved her. She is not only a mentor, advisor, and momma, but she is also my very best friend.

My dad, who exemplifies the heart of my heavenly Father in a way that can only be done when being led by the Spirit. He is passionate about sharing the gospel and leading others to know Jesus, and he has played a major role in shaping me and leading me to be the woman of God that I am today.

My brother, Nolan, who lives in the hope of Jesus and is one of the best leaders that I know. I look up to this young man and his sweet spirit so much.

My mentor, Lisa Long—who is like a second momma to me and listens with care and asks questions that lead me to seek God more and find more of Him—is near and dear to my heart. She helps me voice vision, and her love overflows more and more. She laughs in a way that is fearless about what is to come.

Xochi Dixon, my writing coach, who prayed over me and taught me so much and rejoiced with me as we talked through FaceTime throughout my entire senior year, looking to the Lord for the words to write and how to write them. The joy of the Lord is her strength, and I simply adore her.

All of my friends! My goodness gracious, countless pages would be written if I were to write out each of their names, but the friendships that the Lord has given me have inspired the pages of this book. From meeting at IHOP, getting giddy about what God was doing, to staying up late at sleepovers, dreaming about all that God had in store, I am so thankful for the priceless people who have helped me and believed in the Lord with me.

My team at Tyndale, who sought the Lord regarding this book, and whether they turn to the right or to the left in their decision making, they do so because they are following the voice of the Lord. They welcomed me in with the hospitality of Jesus, and whatever they do, whether in word or in deed, they do it all for the glory of the Lord.

ABOUT THE AUTHOR

EMMA MAE JENKINS is a twenty-year-old lover of Jesus and people. The color yellow, smiling, and flowers are some of her favorite things. She is the daughter of Jason and Amanda Jenkins and the older sister of her brother, Nolan Jenkins. Emma attends Liberty University in Lynchburg, Virginia, and majors in Women's Christian Leadership. Out of an overflow of God's love, she travels throughout the country speaking at conferences and retreats to be a messenger of God's Word. The Lord has blessed Emma with platforms of influence to glorify Him through social media and YouTube. Walking in obedience to these opportunities, she is able to invest in the lives of thousands worldwide.